Exploring the SEASHORE
in Southern Africa

Written and illustrated by
Margo Branch

Photographs by George Branch

Grab this wonderful experience with both hands!

Published by Struik Nature
(an imprint of Penguin Random House South Africa (Pty) Ltd)
Reg. No. 1953/000441/07
The Estuaries No. 4, Oxbow Crescent (off Century Avenue),
Century City, 7441, South Africa
PO Box 1144, Cape Town, 8000 South Africa

Visit www.penguinrandomhouse.co.za and join the Struik Nature Club for updates, news, events and special offers.

First published in in 1987 by Struik Publishers
Second edition published in 1998 by Cambridge University Press
Third edition published in 2018 by Struik Nature

10 9 8 7 6 5 4 3 2 1

Copyright © in text, 1987, 1999, 2018: Margo Branch
Copyright © in photographs, 1987, 1999, 2018: George Branch
Copyright © in illustrations, 1987, 1999, 2018: Margo Branch
Copyright © in published edition, 2018: Penguin Random House South Africa (Pty) Ltd

Publisher: Pippa Parker
Managing editor: Helen de Villiers
Editor: Emily Donaldson
Designers: Janice Evans, Neil Bester
Illustrator: Margo Branch
Proofreader: Thea Grobbelaar

Reproduction by Hirt & Carter Cape (Pty) Ltd
Printed and bound in China by Leo Paper Products Ltd.

All rights reserved. No part of this publication may be reproduced, stored in a retrieval system, or transmitted, in any form or by any means, electronic, mechanical, photocopying, recording or otherwise, without the prior written permission of the copyright owner(s).

Print ISBN: 9781775846277
ePub ISBN: 9781775846284

Acknowledgements

What fun we have had over the years unpacking the wonders of our shoreline with friends and our expanded family – Bryony, Adriaan, Trevor, Ruth, Simon, Patrick, Sam and Miya. We have shared field trips with students and researchers from the coastal universities of Cape Town, KwaZulu-Natal, Rhodes and Nelson Mandela Bay. The staff and volunteer rangers of the South African National Parks and the inspiring members of MCEN (Marine and Coastal Educators Network) have all contributed. My 10 years working at Two Oceans Aquarium in Cape Town provided many opportunities to learn, observe, paint and photograph the underwater world. At Arniston, the late Bertie Jessop taught me the joys of watercolour painting and exploring. A big thank you to the team at Struik Nature and especially Janice Evans who, in 1987, designed the first edition and who has also provided the concept for this fresh new edition.

A handful of treasures can lead to a lifetime of joy.

Contents

Introduction 4

Waves and sand
Floating animals 6
Sandy-shore beach cleaners 8
Be a crab detective 10
Shells 12
Masters of swimming and colour change 14
The octopus and the paper nautilus 16

Rocky-shore intertidal life
The rocky shore and tides 18
Living in a harsh environment 20
Seaweeds and herbivores 22
Why some shells have holes 24
Shellfish and their enemies 26
Rock lobsters and their relatives 28

Rock pools – living under water
Rock pools and camouflage 30
Sea slugs 32
Anemones and corals 34
The sea stars 36
Urchins and sea cucumbers 38
Danger 40

Diving deeper
The kelp forest 42
Plankton and red tides 44
Fish and fisheries 46
Strange and important fish 48
Tropical fish – an explosion of colour 50
Sharks, rays and skates 52
Sea birds 54
Marine mammals 56

The bigger picture
Contrasting life in two oceans 58
Conservation 60
Useful contacts and references 62
Key words 63
Index 64

Introduction

Many living treasures occur along southern Africa's coastline. Some float or swim in the sea; others dig themselves into the sand or cling to the rocks. Our shores are bathed by two oceans – the warm Indian Ocean to the east, with its many bright tropical animals, and the cold Atlantic Ocean to the west, with its vast kelp forests and huge shoals of silver fish. Rich and fascinating life occurs wherever the land meets the sea, because the constantly changing tides, currents, wind, waves and sunlight create many different habitats.

Let's dive in now and peer through our goggles at the magical life beneath these waters, then lift our eyes and watch dolphins leaping and seagulls soaring – or maybe even a whale blowing! All of these living things depend on one another and belong to a finely balanced ecosystem, which we should help to conserve.

Did you know?

Your best pieces of beach equipment are your eyes and your enquiring mind. It is difficult to keep sea creatures alive in captivity, so rather watch them where they live and leave them there for visiting again.

Put on your sunscreen and come and explore.

Waves and sand

Floating animals

After a storm, floating animals wash up on the beach. Look out for bluebottles, by-the-wind sailors, bubble-raft shells and jellyfish.

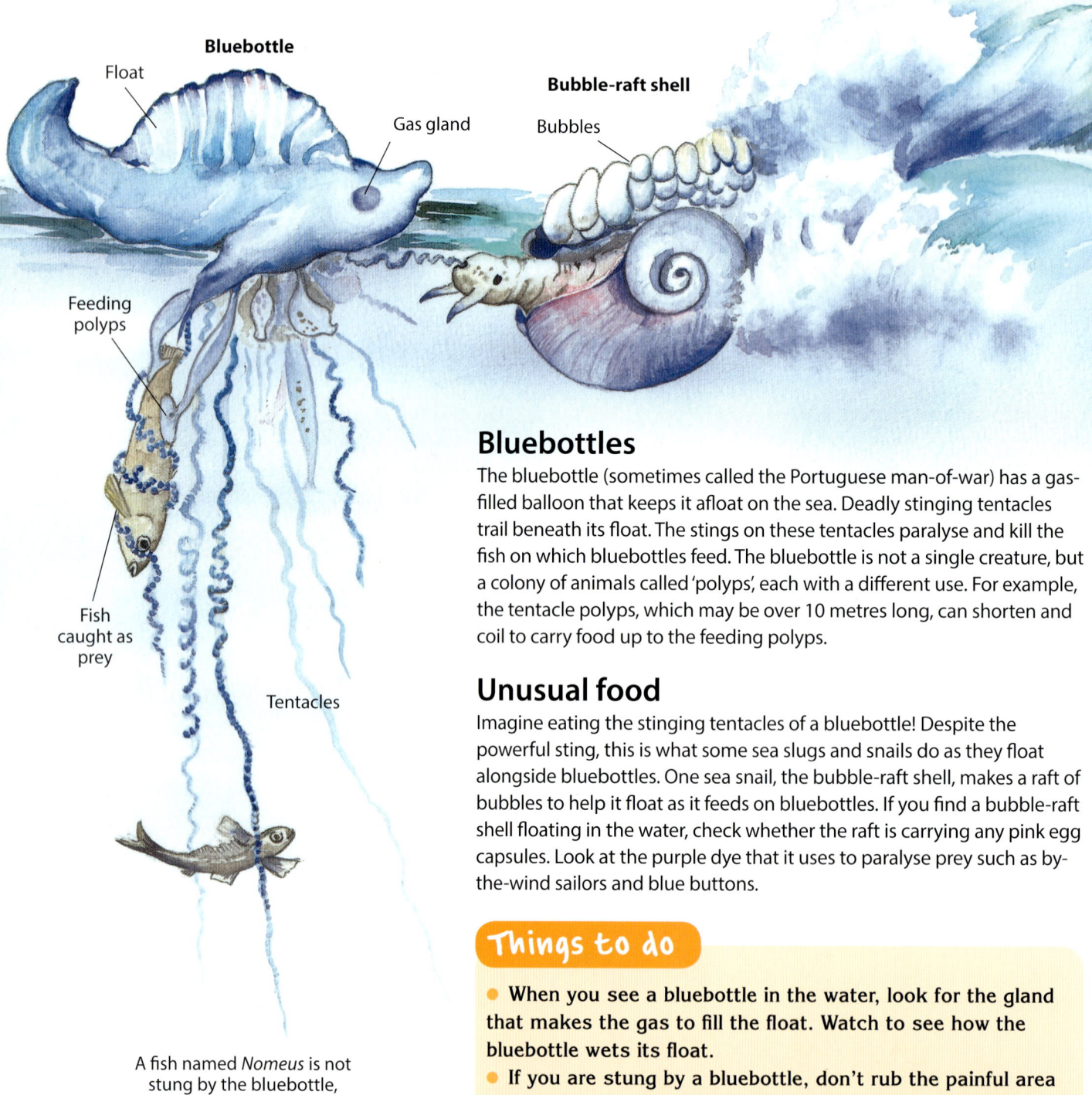

A fish named *Nomeus* is not stung by the bluebottle, and shelters unharmed among the tentacles, safe from larger fish.

Bluebottles

The bluebottle (sometimes called the Portuguese man-of-war) has a gas-filled balloon that keeps it afloat on the sea. Deadly stinging tentacles trail beneath its float. The stings on these tentacles paralyse and kill the fish on which bluebottles feed. The bluebottle is not a single creature, but a colony of animals called 'polyps', each with a different use. For example, the tentacle polyps, which may be over 10 metres long, can shorten and coil to carry food up to the feeding polyps.

Unusual food

Imagine eating the stinging tentacles of a bluebottle! Despite the powerful sting, this is what some sea slugs and snails do as they float alongside bluebottles. One sea snail, the bubble-raft shell, makes a raft of bubbles to help it float as it feeds on bluebottles. If you find a bubble-raft shell floating in the water, check whether the raft is carrying any pink egg capsules. Look at the purple dye that it uses to paralyse prey such as by-the-wind sailors and blue buttons.

Things to do

- When you see a bluebottle in the water, look for the gland that makes the gas to fill the float. Watch to see how the bluebottle wets its float.
- If you are stung by a bluebottle, don't rub the painful area with sand or wash it in fresh water. Instead, remove any pieces of tentacle and wash your skin carefully with salty water. Then soak it in very hot water to relieve the pain. Severe cases are rare but should be treated by a doctor.

> **Things to do**
>
> Collect animals washed up after a storm and float them in a rock pool or clear container filled with sea water. Can you work out why they are blue or colourless?

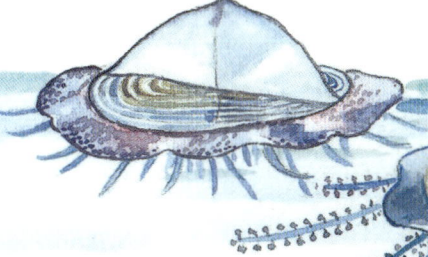

By-the-wind sailor

Blue button

Rafts to float

The by-the-wind sailor has a delicate air-filled raft with a sail above it, and short stinging tentacles and feeding polyps beneath the raft. The circular floating raft of the blue button, *Porpita*, lacks a sail but has beautifully branched tentacles. Neither of these creatures has a sting that is harmful to humans.

Jellyfish

Transparent jellyfish are almost invisible either to their enemies or to the tiny creatures on which they feed. They swim by contracting and expanding their umbrella-like bell. In the centre of the bell is the mouth, surrounded by frilly lips. There are four pouches underneath the bell, where the eggs are formed. Most jellyfish are harmless to humans. The box jellyfish, however, has four long tentacles and gives a venomous sting. It is related to a deadly Australian jellyfish, the sea wasp.

Box jellyfish

Tentacles

Frilly lips

Egg pouch

Compass jellyfish feed on plankton and small fish.

Common root-mouthed jellyfish grow up to 1.5m wide.

Small mouths

Sea swallows use second-hand stings

The sea swallow is not a bird but a beautiful sea slug about 2 centimetres long. It has wing-like flaps that spread out to help it float on the sea. It uses the stings of the bluebottles upon which it feeds in an unusual way. The stinging cells travel through the gut of the sea swallow without causing any damage. They then pass to the surface of the sea slug's skin, where they are used as second-hand stinging weapons.

Sea swallows are small but quite common in summer; you might spot them in the waves or stranded on the sandy beach.

Waves and sand

Sandy-shore beach cleaners

The sandy beach may look empty, but many small creatures are hiding in the sand, safe from the sun and the birds. They clean up what the sea washes onto the beach.

Scavenging **kelp gulls** help to keep the beach clean by gobbling up dead animals.

Plough shells

Plough shells feed on dead or dying animals washed up on the beach. They crawl out of the sand at low tide, pump up their large feet with water and surf up the shore with the waves. They land at the waterline along with other floating animals on which they feed. Plough shells are able to smell minuscule quantities of substances that dissolve into the water when an animal's body decays. This means they can sense exactly where dead animals are and plough their way straight towards them. However, if they sense a live shark or ray in the water nearby, they burrow quickly into the sand to escape being eaten. As high tide approaches they bury themselves so that they are not stranded high on the beach by a large wave.

Things to do

Pick up a plough shell and prod beneath it. Note how it squirts water out of its foot so that its foot is small enough to be tucked away inside the shell.

White mussels

The white mussel is usually hidden in the sand. It has two tubes called siphons, which it extends into the water. Through one siphon it sucks water and gathers the plankton with its gills. The filtered water is then pumped out through the second siphon. If the mussel doesn't pull its siphons back into the shell quickly enough, fish sometimes nip off their ends. Small white mussels move up and down the shore with the tide.

Above: A **plough shell** surfs up the beach.
Below: **Plough shells** feast on a bluebottle.

Sandy-shore birds

Little white-fronted plovers seem to twinkle over the sand on their dainty feet as they search for food. They use their pointed beaks to probe for beach hoppers on which to feast. Their eggs and chicks are so well camouflaged in their nests on the beach that you could easily step on them by mistake.

Things to do
- Watch white-fronted plovers.
- Can you find an open nest on the sand? Look above the high-tide level and follow the bird's footprints to areas behind bits of debris. Don't disturb the nest.

Night-time gang

After dark, a gang of tiny beach cleaners gets to work. Beach hoppers and sea lice patiently chew up mountains of kelp and other seaweeds. There can be up to 25,000 beach hoppers in an area the size of your towel. During the day they burrow into the sand, where it is cool and damp. They come out at night when the tide is low. They have an internal 'biological clock' to keep them on time.

White-fronted plover

Things to do
- Lift up a piece of kelp and scratch in the sand beaneath it – what lives there?
- At low tide one night, use your torch to look for the 'clean-up gang'.

Kelp

Remember to pick up plastic, bottles and metal cans and place them in a bin for recycling.

The 'clean-up gang': a group of **beach hoppers** and a **sea louse** (white arrow) seen at night with a torch

Waves and sand

Be a crab detective

Crabs have a hard protective shell that allows them to live successfully in all sorts of places. The shell, which is really an outer skeleton, has joints that let the legs bend, so that the crab can walk, swim, climb and dig. A small, jointed tail is folded under the crab's body. Eggs are attached to the female's tail and look like tiny red or black berries.

Male fiddler crabs have one larger, more brightly coloured nipper, which they wave to attract mates. These crabs live in mangrove swamps.

Crabs grow out of their shells

As a crab grows, it gets too big for its shell and must moult. The shell splits and the crab climbs out, leaving behind a perfect – but too small – set of armour. The soft crab pumps itself up with water to expand its body, so that when its skin hardens to form a new shell, it is a few sizes bigger. For a few days, while the shell is soft, the crab cannot run and is in great danger of being eaten by birds, squid and fish, so it must hide away.

Things to do

Be a crab detective. Inspect crabs for clues to work out how they live. Look at their limbs. Can you imagine why crabs run sideways?

Swimmers

The back legs of swimming crabs are paddle-shaped for swimming. When a crab sinks to the floor of the sea, it also uses these paddles to flick sand over its flat body to hide itself. Fine hairs widen the paddles for swimming, and hairs on the body keep sand out of the gill chambers. The body of the three-spot swimming crab is sandy in colour, with red spots. Sharp spines on the edge of the shell and strong nippers protect the crab against attack. The nippers are powerful enough to break open tasty plough shells and white mussels. So if you are sorting through the creatures in a trek net, be careful of the swimming crabs' nippers.

A **three-spot swimming crab** eats a plough shell.

Paddle-shaped back leg

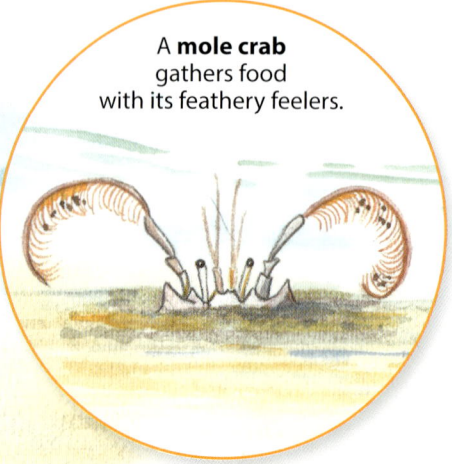

A **mole crab** gathers food with its feathery feelers.

Ghost crab

Things to do
If you are on the east coast, you can watch ghost crabs at dusk and dawn. As they are very shy, you may need binoculars to watch them from a distance.

Ghosts
During the day ghost crabs stay cool, moist and safe in their burrows beneath the sand. At dusk they creep out, hoist their eyes, which are stalked for long-distance vision, and scurry off to collect food washed up by the sea. They use their strong nippers to crush shells and tear up food. Like pale ghosts, the crabs appear and disappear suddenly: they sprint along the shore on their long, pointed legs and then vanish sideways down a burrow. Their eyes fold into special grooves, and the box-shaped body fits easily into the burrow. They guard the entrance with one large nipper. Water can be stored in chambers on the sides of the body so that the crab can use its gills to breathe at low tide, when it is out of the water.

Things to do
Search the beach for crab shells: remember these are not dead crabs, but the shells that have been left behind after moulting. Can you tell from these shells what sort of crabs have moulted recently and live hidden nearby?

A surfing crab
The mole crab cannot walk. Instead its barrel-shaped body is rolled up and down the beach by the waves. Its front legs are like spades, which it uses to dig itself backwards into the sand. The back legs are long and thin and end in small nippers, which reach inside the gill chambers to remove sand from the gills. It has long feelers, with a fringe of hairs, which it holds in the water like a net to trap small particles of food. It then curls its feelers under its mouthparts and eats the trapped food.

Things to do
You can try to catch a mole crab by holding a hand-net in the breakers at the water's edge in KwaZulu-Natal. Once you've examined the mole crab, release it at the edge of the waves.

A barrel-shaped **mole crab** surfs up the beach.

Waves and sand

Shells

It is fun to collect shells that wash up on the beach. They have beautiful colours and shapes and will remind you of your adventures at the seashore.

Sort the shells you find on the beach into the groups shown on this page:
- **Chitons** have a tough, leathery foot and eight overlapping shell plates that look like a coat of armour. The end shell plate often looks like a set of false teeth.
- **Bivalves** have two shells that fit together tightly. They have no head, and filter particles of food out of the water using their gills.
- **Ear shells** are ear-shaped with a wide opening.
- **Limpets** are flat, cone-shaped shells with a wide opening.
- **Winkles** have coiled shells with a round opening. There are many different types of winkle, and they eat plant material.
- **Cowries** are shiny, egg-shaped shells with long, narrow openings.
- **Whelks** are usually spiralled and pointed, and have an oval shell opening with a notch or long groove. They feed on dead or live animals and have a tube that sticks out through the groove in the shell to taste the water for any food. There are many different types of whelk.
- **Bubble shells** are the very fragile shells that belong to the few sea slugs that have shells (see page 32). They are different from bubble-raft shells (see page 6).
- **Cephalopods** include the octopus, which has no shell, squid, ram's-horn squid and cuttlefish, which have internal shells, and the paper nautilus, in which the female builds a delicate shell.

Chitons

Bivalves

Ear shells

Limpets

Molluscs

Molluscs are soft-bodied animals like snails, slugs and cuttlefish. They usually have a head, a foot and a hump containing the body organs. A special skirt of skin called the mantle covers the animal and encloses its gills. In many molluscs the mantle secretes a hard shell of lime; the inside glistens with beautiful mother-of-pearl, but the outside layer is furry or horny and can be peeled off. Colour taken from their food is used to pattern the shell; some shells, for instance, look and smell like the seaweeds on which the animal feeds.

Things to do

- Label shells you have collected, noting where and when you collected them. You can add their names later when you have identified the shells.
- Visit a museum that has a shell collection. Compare shells that have been collected from different parts of the country. Which ones come from the warm waters of KwaZulu-Natal? Which ones come from the cold west coast?
- Try to find living molluscs and watch what they do. Some sit on the open rocks, but others hide under stones and seaweeds or dig into the sand.

Things NOT to do!

Never be greedy about taking live shells, either for your collection or to eat.

Did you know?

Cephalopods are molluscs that can swim. Cephalopod means 'head foot' – they have a large head and instead of a flat foot, they have 10 or 12 tentacles with suckers (see pages 14–17).

Cephalopods

Bubble shells

Whelks

Winkles

Cowries

Waves and sand

Squid have eight arms and two long tentacles with suckers.

Siphon

Masters of swimming and colour change

The octopus and its relatives – the paper nautilus, squid, cuttlefish and ram's-horn squid – are amazing molluscs that have left the seafloor. They belong to a mollusc group called the cephalopods and, unlike snails, they can swim. Cuttlefish and squid, in particular, are masterful swimmers: they can move very quickly to escape attack or to catch fish.

Jet propulsion

Both squid and cuttlefish swim slowly by gently rippling the flat fins that run along each side of the body. However, when they need to escape, they have siphons through which they can squirt water to propel themselves backwards at great speed. (Their close relative the octopus lacks fins, but is also able to use jet propulsion.)

Internal surfboards

Unlike many molluscs, cephalopods lack a hard outer shell. Cuttlefish, for example, have a flat, internal shell, shaped like a surfboard. The shell is very light and filled with air spaces, which help it float. Squid have only a thin horny internal shell.

Survival strategies

To confuse their enemies while they escape, squid, cuttlefish and their relatives squirt a cloud of ink into the water. The ink's rich brown colour (used in the painting above) is called sepia. This is also the scientific name for the cuttlefish. In the past, cuttlefish ink was used for writing and painting. Cephalopods can instantly change colour to match the background – these changes are especially beautiful in the squid and cuttlefish. Their stripes ripple like the water that passes over them. They also use vivid colour changes to attract their mates.

A **cuttlefish** using its two long tentacles to capture a sand shrimp

The **cuttlefish's** black eggs are fastened to seaweed with loops.

Sand shrimps can change colour.

Cuttlefish shell

Ink

> **Things to do**
>
> Look for squid when fishermen haul in their trek nets.

Squid

Squid are among the largest invertebrates (animals without backbones) in the sea. Giant deep-sea squid can be over 10 metres long, and leave huge sucker marks on sperm whales that eat them.

Ram's-horn shell

Spirula – it is rare to find a live animal; only a handful of people have ever seen one.

A floating spiral shell

You will often find ram's-horn shells washed up on the beach. They are the internal shells of a deep-sea animal called the ram's-horn squid or *Spirula*, which floats along with its head down. The shell provides it with buoyancy.

> **Did you know?**
>
> The calamari that we eat comes from squid. A simple way to cook calamari is to remove the guts and shell, slice the flesh and shake it in a bag of flour, then dip the pieces in beaten egg and fry them quickly, seasoning with salt.

> **Things to do**
>
> Look for white cuttlefish shells washed up on the beach. These shells are given to budgies to nibble on, as the calcium they contain helps build strong bones.

Food chain

Squid move in large shoals. They are important food for fish, whales, seals and dolphins. Squid and cuttlefish capture shrimps, crabs and small fish with their arms and tentacles, and crunch them up with a horny beak inside the mouth. Have you noticed the food chain in the book so far? Look back and see:

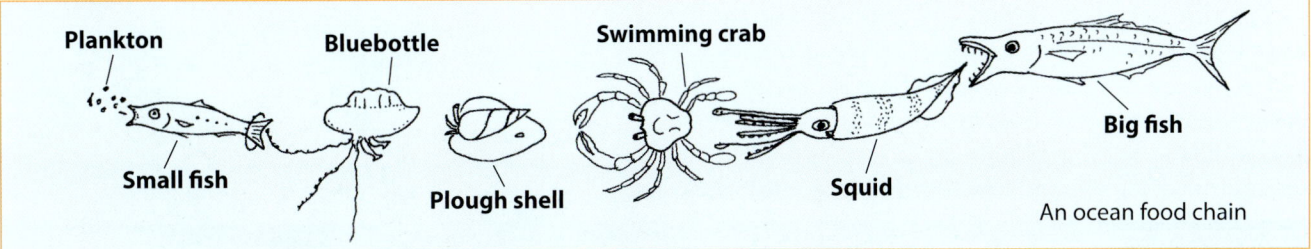

An ocean food chain

Waves and sand

The octopus and the paper nautilus

The name cephalopods was chosen from the Greek words for 'head' and 'foot', because most of the animal is made up of a large head and a 'foot', which is divided into eight or 10 long arms that surround the mouth. This body shape is particularly obvious in the octopus and paper nautilus.

The female **paper nautilus** carries her eggs in a floating shell.

Cephalopods

As we've seen, cephalopods are not confined to the seafloor or rocks, like other molluscs are, and can swim by squirting water out of their bodies. The cuttlefish, paper nautilus and ram's-horn squid also have shells filled with air spaces for buoyancy.

Because they are active, cephalopods have large brains to coordinate their movements. They use their well-developed eyes and their arms, which are equipped with suckers, to find and capture prey. The body is a muscular bag filled with organs and has a cavity for the gills. Water is sucked into the cavity and flows over the gills. Cephalopods breathe much like fish: in the gills, oxygen from the water passes into the blood, and waste gas is removed and squirted out of the siphon. Unlike fish though, cephalopods have blue blood running in their veins.

Things to do

To find a paper nautilus shell, try to be the first visitor to the beach after a windy night in autumn. You may have to look while it is still dark, before gulls and shell collectors arrive.

Paper nautilus

The paper nautilus looks like a pale octopus riding in one of the most beautiful and highly prized shells in the ocean. Only the female builds a shell. She is joined there by a tiny male. After they have mated, she lays thousands of eggs, which stick to the inside of the shell. As they float along, she cares for the eggs by blowing water over them to give them oxygen. The paper nautilus eats fish and other small animals.

The clever octopus

The octopus is probably the cleverest of all the invertebrates. It learns quickly and easily to recognize shapes and colours. It has wonderful eyes that are very like ours, and it has a good sense of balance. The octopus lives in pools and glides over rocks on its eight suckered arms, feeling along ledges and cracks for hidden food such as shells and crabs. It grabs unsuspecting crabs and bites them with its powerful beak, killing its prey with its poisonous saliva. When angry or in danger, an octopus can change colour instantly. If threatened, it can squeeze through spaces as small as its eye or swim rapidly and escape behind an inky screen. One of its main enemies is the moray eel (see page 29).

A good mother

When octopuses mate, the male uses a special long arm to place packets of sperm into the female's mantle cavity. There the sperm fertilizes her thousands of eggs. She lays the eggs and they hang, like bunches of tiny, pale grapes, from the wall of the cave where she lives. She is a good mother, protecting her eggs, blowing water over them and keeping them clean. The tiny, transparent youngsters hatch after about 40 days and reach adulthood within a year. Common octopuses don't live very long – just one or two years.

Things to do

- Explore pools with rocks. Can you find an octopus? You'll often see piles of shells and stones near the entrance to an octopus lair.
- Dangle something orange nearby. If you're lucky, the octopus may think it is a crab and be lured into the open. However, an octopus is not very easily fooled!

If you notice a rock crab climbing out of a pool, check to see if an octopus is chasing it.

Rock crab

Eggs

Octopus

Rocky–shore intertidal life

The rocky shore and tides

Each day and each night there is a high tide when the water rises high on the shore. These are followed, six hours later, by low tides, when water recedes, exposing an area known as the intertidal zone. Marine life that lives in this zone can be seen at low tide.

Spring and neap tides

Every two weeks there are extra-high and extra-low tides known as spring tides. Low spring tide is the best time to visit a rocky shore because many exciting animals are uncovered.

What causes the tides?

Tides are caused by the gravitational pull of the moon and the sun. At new moon and full moon, the sun and the moon are lined up and pull together, which causes the very high and very low spring tides. In South Africa low spring tide occurs at about nine o'clock in the morning and evening. Each day after this the tides occur about 50 minutes later, so that after a week, the low tides take place at about three o'clock in the morning and afternoon. At that time you will see a half-moon and, because the sun and the moon are then pulling at right angles to one another, the tides are neither very high nor very low and are called neap tides.

Things to do

- Keep a record of the times of high and low tide for a week or a month and see how they change.
- Note how the phases of the moon affect the time and height of the tide.
- Find out the times of the tides from the weather bulletin in the newspaper or the internet. See if you can predict the time of low spring tide for your next visit to the beach.

Which animals live at which tide levels?

Different animals live in distinct zones at different tide levels, and can indicate to us how high or low the tide is at a particular time. For example, if the water reaches to the zone where barnacles occur, we know it is mid-tide.

High-tide level

If you explore a rocky shore at high tide, the only live shells you are likely to find are hundreds of tiny periwinkles. There are so many that they seem to litter the rocks! Hardy lichens form beautiful coloured crusts on the rocks. They are a partnership between a plant and a fungus.

Mid-tide level

When the tide starts going out, other creatures are uncovered. At mid-tide there are plenty of barnacles, making the rocks rough to walk on. There are also limpets and winkles. On the east coast near Durban you can see oysters cemented to the rocks. When the water drops lower, look at the mussels, worm tubes, sponges and spiny sea urchins. In KwaZulu-Natal, remember to take care as you walk over the green anemone-like zoanthids. If you are in the Western Cape, be careful as there are many slippery seaweeds.

Low-tide level

At low tide you can see many more seaweeds of different types. Some are really beautiful, and their purples, blues and greens sparkle in the sun. Others, called corallines, are hard and jointed. Many tiny creatures live among the seaweeds. On the south coast, look out for pear limpets at this level. Redbait animals, which are only exposed at low spring tide, are sometimes called sea squirts. Watch them squirt water as they contract their bodies.

Always be careful – look out for big waves when the tide starts to rise again.

Zones of life at each tide level

This photograph, taken at low spring tide, shows the side of a granite rock on the west coast near Cape Town. You can clearly see that different zones of life occur at each tide level.

High-tide level – at spring tide
Periwinkles

High-tide level – at neap tide
Barnacles and limpets

Mid-tide level
Barnacles, seaweeds, limpets and winkles

Low-tide level – at neap tide
Mixed community plus redbait

Low-tide level – at spring tide
Diverse marine seaweeds, corallines and redbait

Things to do

On the east coast, near Durban, the zones of life on a rocky shore stretch out along a flattish slope extending for many metres. If you are visiting the east coast, look at each tide level and see whether you can find some of the east-coast creatures shown below.

Three kinds of periwinkles living at the **high-tide level**

A crab sheltering among oysters at the **mid-tide level**

A bubble shell, slippery zoanthids and a bright red sponge living at **mid-tide level**

Brightly coloured seaweeds at the **low-tide level**. Three different animals are hiding in the seaweed. Can you spot them?

Rocky-shore intertidal life

Living in a harsh environment

Animals living on a rocky shore have to be adaptable to survive both in and out of water. When they are exposed at low tide on a hot, windy day, they are in danger of roasting or drying out. At high tide, rough waves can damage them or wash them away. Active animals can escape from danger and hardship, while barnacles and slow-moving snails and worms live in hard shells or tubes for protection.

High and dry

Only animals that are really tough can live on the upper part of the rocky shore. Tiny periwinkles, for example, are resilient and manage to survive out of water for many hours. They crawl into cool cracks and cluster together to shade one another and to save moisture. If it is too hot to stand on the rocks, they hang from threads of dried slime and seal up the openings to their shells. Although the waves are not strong high on the shore, food is in short supply. Periwinkles feed on the thin black lichen that coats the rocks. Considering their harsh environment, it is little wonder that they are so small and grow very slowly.

Tiny hardy periwinkles hang from slime threads.

Things to do

Visit the same rocks at different times: when it is hot and dry, when it is cool and moist, at low tide and at high tide. Observe how the shelled animals behave under different conditions.

Wet and dry

The granular limpet lives a bit lower on the shore, with the barnacles. It can still be hot here, but these animals are able to spend more time under water keeping cool. The limpet's conical shell is pale and knobbly and doesn't get as hot as a smooth dark shell would. It fits the rock exactly to give a watertight seal. The waves are stronger at this level, and the limpet's muscular foot grips the rock firmly when the waves batter the shore. The limpet scrapes the rock bare of seaweeds and then has to wander in search of more food – but it must be able to find its way back to exactly the same place, where its shell fits the rock. Scientists have puzzled over how limpets do this. Usually they follow their slime trails back. However, they can find their way to their home 'scars' even if they are lifted and moved a short distance from their trails!

Limpets, barnacles and tube worms shelter in shells or tubes, protected from the sun and waves.

Barnacle larva

Barnacle feeding

An oystercatcher can eat 5,000 limpets in a year.

Oystercatchers

Oystercatchers strut over the rocks on their red legs. They jab limpets off the rocks with their flat, red beak and can open and eat mussels. Where there are many oystercatchers, few limpets survive and a rich carpet of seaweeds grows on the rocks.

Things to do

- Observe oystercatchers through binoculars and try to count how many limpets or mussels they eat.
- Search an area where the birds have been feeding and collect the shells. Which type of shelled animals do they prefer?

Fixed for life and filter feeding

Acorn barnacles, mussels and reef worms don't risk getting lost: their shells are glued to the rock. They have to rely on food delivered by the waves. When water flows over a barnacle the plates at the top of the shell open and two fans of hairy legs comb the water. Small pieces of food are caught in this net. Tube worms also use feathery fans to filter feed. Mussels and oysters have two shells that clamp together so that their bodies are safely sealed inside. They open their shells and suck in water from which they filter out little bits of food (see page 44).

The eggs of these animals hatch into young called larvae that swim in the sea. Larvae are able to move to new areas, but it is important that they choose a suitable place to settle and grow into adults, as a bad choice, with a poor supply of food, could mean death. They are attracted to places where others of their kind are already living. Once there, they space themselves out so that they do not crowd their neighbours.

Things to do

- How many different types of barnacles, mussels and tube worms can you find?
- Watch these creatures feeding when they are covered by water.

Tail

The **reef worm** lives in a sandy tube. Its tail loops up to eject waste products out of the tube.

Barnacles, reef worms, brown mussels and sandy anemones compete for space.

Rocky-shore intertidal life

Seaweeds and herbivores

Seaweeds, glistening in rich greens, reds and browns, feed and shelter many sea creatures. They are known as primary producers, because they produce the plant food eaten by grazers and herbivores, which are in turn eaten by predators higher up the food chain.

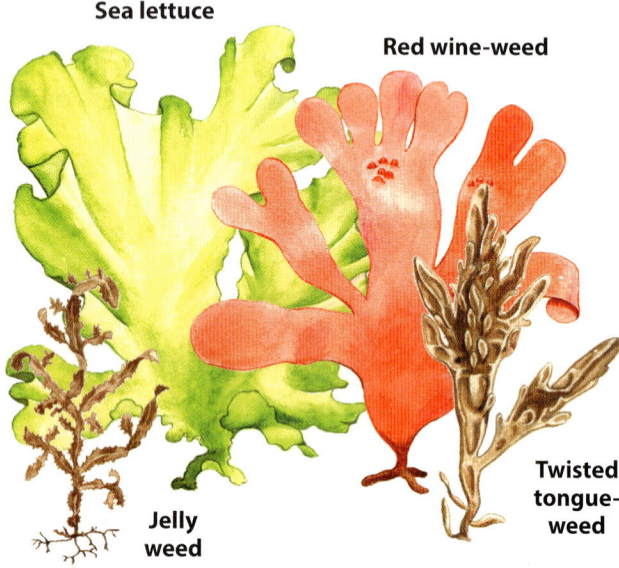

Sea lettuce

Red wine-weed

Jelly weed

Twisted tongue-weed

Seaweeds

Seaweeds are simple plants and, like land plants, can make their own food. Their leaves contain chloroplasts, special structures full of chlorophyll, a chemical that captures sunlight and produces food energy (by photosynthesis). However, seaweeds are adapted for life in the sea and differ from land plants in various ways. Land plants need roots to anchor themselves in the ground and to take up water and minerals from the soil, but seaweeds don't. Supported by the water, they can simply attach themselves directly to rocks or sand, and the entire surface of the plant absorbs water and minerals straight from the sea. Also, unlike land plants, seaweeds don't produce flowers or seeds; instead, they reproduce by releasing tiny spores.

Adaptable seaweeds

In calm water seaweeds often have large, flat fronds ideal for absorbing light and nutrients, but where there are waves or currents seaweeds have split, flexible fronds, which flow with the water to avoid being shredded. Where the waves crash onto the rocks only tough branching seaweeds and low-growing crusts can survive by clinging tightly to the rocks.

Green sea lettuce can tolerate a wide range of salt concentrations and may be found where fresh water pours into the sea, or in tidal pools, which may be diluted when it rains, or become very salty on hot days, as the water evaporates.

Dead man's fingers: wet and dry

Tide in: The fingers are swollen, jelly-filled and wet.

Tide out: Water is lost from the jelly inside, and the living skin is wrinkled but not damaged.

Purple laver is an edible seaweed.

Things to do

- Purple laver lives high on the shore and looks like black plastic when dry. Measure the length of a dry plant, then wet it thoroughly and measure it again. It has a jelly-like layer that swells with water.
- On a hot day look for the salt crystals that form when small pools dry out.

Herbivores

Many molluscs, sea urchins and fish are herbivores and eat only seaweeds. Winkles, chitons and limpets have flat tongues with rows of teeth – you may see the rasp marks they leave on seaweeds. The abalone or perlemoen eats kelp plants. It lifts up the front of its shell and clamps down on pieces of drift kelp as they are swept past by the waves. Then it can munch away for hours.

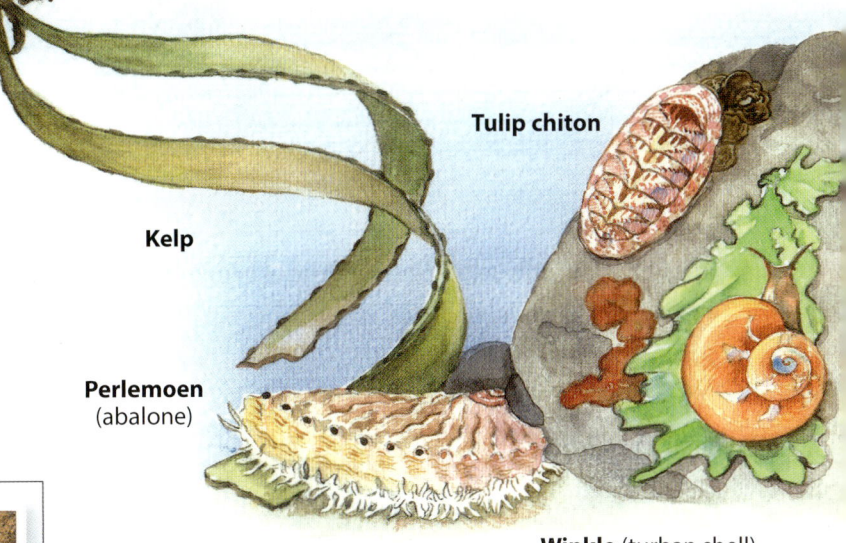

An experiment

Limpets were kept out of this square on the rocks by poisonous red paint that they could not cross. Seaweeds soon grew in the protected square, providing a sharp contrast to the bare rock surrounding the antifouling paint, where the limpets continued to graze. If people harvest too many grazers, the seashore soon becomes overgrown with seaweeds.

Gardening limpets

The pear limpet lives in rough waves low on the shore. It can't leave its home scar for fear of being washed away. Instead of scraping the rock bare of all food, it helps fine red seaweeds to grow in a little garden around it. The limpet nibbles only the tops of the seaweeds, like mowing a quick-growing lawn, and never uses up its supply of food. Young limpets make their homes on the backs of bigger ones. These gardeners are so successful that they form a solid band low on the shore.

Long-spined limpets change their diet as they grow: the tiny limpets feed on a brown seaweed that coats the shells of winkles. When they grow too big for the winkle they have to move off and make do with a diet of a different kind of seaweed that looks like white paint on the rocks. Eventually the limpets get big enough to protect their own gardens of brown crust-like seaweed, and they push away any intruding grazers that try to steal a bite.

Things to do

- How many pear limpets can you count in a square metre?
- Find large, small and tiny long-spined limpets on their different gardens.

Catching the light

To photosynthesize and supply themselves with food, plants need sunlight. Some have air bladders that help them to float up towards the light. The green caulerpa seaweed often gets swamped with sand, leaving just the tips of its leaves exposed, so its chloroplasts can move into these exposed bits to make the most of the available light. They can also move away from the seaweed's surface to protect the plant from burning when the light is too harsh.

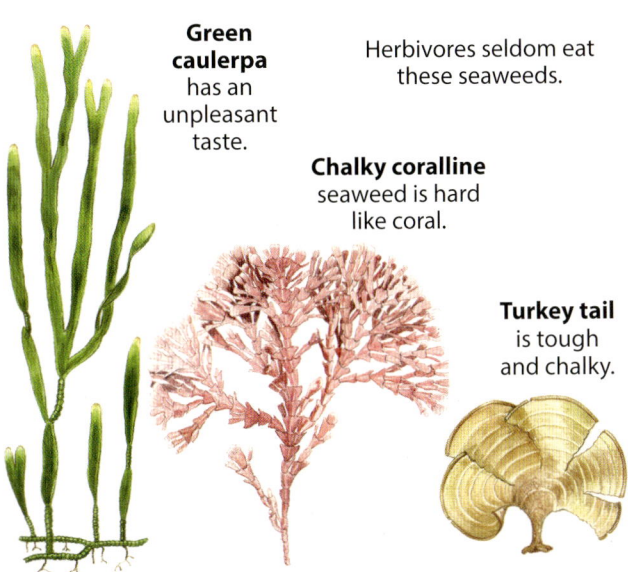

Green caulerpa has an unpleasant taste.

Herbivores seldom eat these seaweeds.

Chalky coralline seaweed is hard like coral.

Turkey tail is tough and chalky.

Pear limpets and long-spined limpets on their gardens.

Rocky-shore intertidal life

Why some shells have holes

If shells protect the soft snail inside, why do some shells have holes? Have a close look at the shells you have collected on the beach. There are two types of shell that always have holes: ear shells and keyhole limpets. Others sometimes have holes that have been drilled by predators.

Shells that use holes for breathing

The holes in a keyhole limpet or Venus ear shell are used to direct water out of the shell. In both creatures, clean water enters at the front of the shell, bringing life-giving oxygen to the gills. It then passes out through the holes of the ear shell, or via the chimney-like tube projecting from the top of the limpet, flushing waste material and eggs into the sea. In this way clean incoming water is separated from dirty outgoing water. As the Venus ear shell grows, the wastewater holes at the back edge of the shell are filled in and new ones form.

Because of the hole in its shell, the keyhole limpet is at risk of drying out and cannot survive in the open. It occurs low on the shore, hiding under rocks by day, and emerging at night to feed. In fact, the shell is too small to protect the body. It covers only the gills, and looks like a little cap on the limpet's back. The shell of the mantled keyhole limpet is even more reduced – it lies under the skin of the slug-like animal.

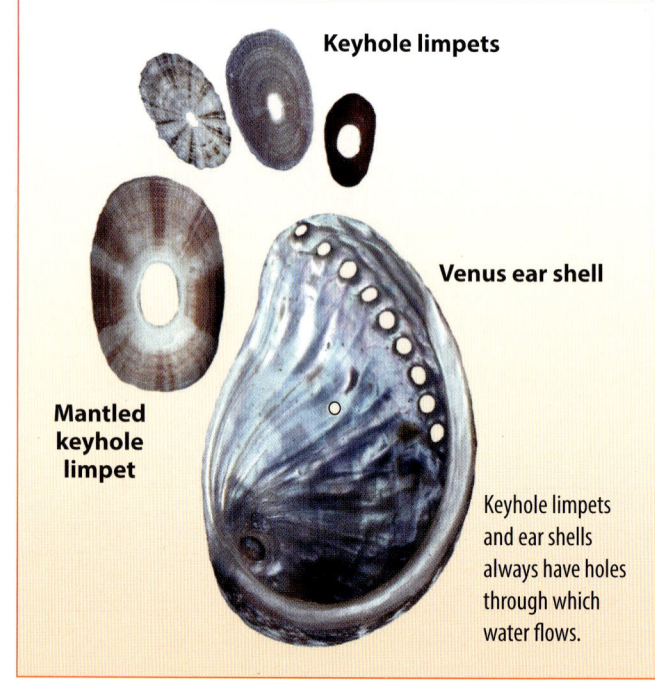

Keyhole limpets

Venus ear shell

Mantled keyhole limpet

Keyhole limpets and ear shells always have holes through which water flows.

The helmet shell, like other whelks, does not have holes in its shell. Instead, it extends a tube through a groove in the opening of its shell to test for the scent of food. It sucks water in through the tube and expels dirty water at the side of the head.

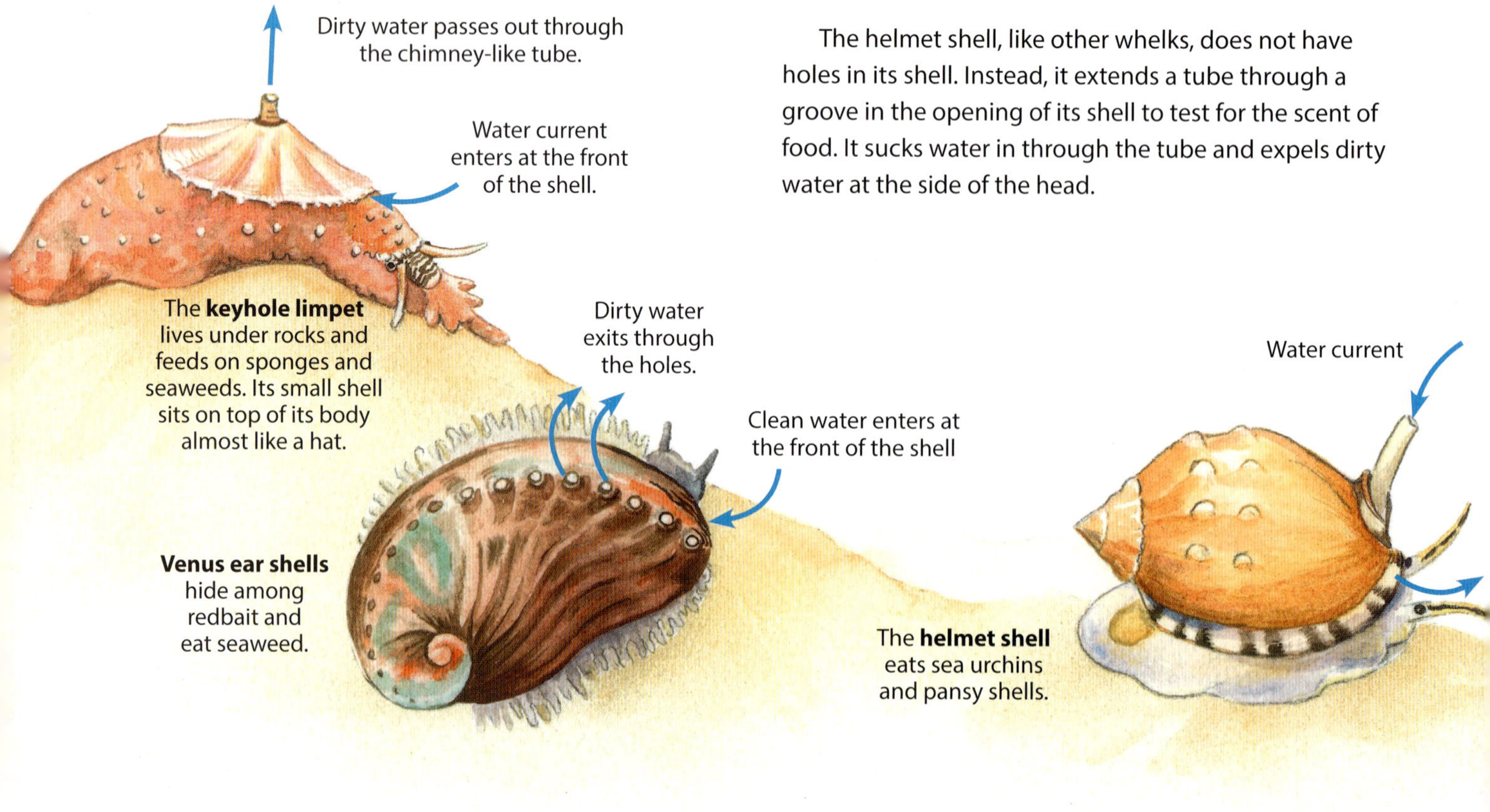

Dirty water passes out through the chimney-like tube.

Water current enters at the front of the shell.

The **keyhole limpet** lives under rocks and feeds on sponges and seaweeds. Its small shell sits on top of its body almost like a hat.

Dirty water exits through the holes.

Clean water enters at the front of the shell

Venus ear shells hide among redbait and eat seaweed.

Water current

The **helmet shell** eats sea urchins and pansy shells.

> **Things to do**
>
> Drop some bait into a rock pool and watch scavenging whelks attack it.

Holes drilled by whelks

Holes in other shells are usually a sign that the animal has been killed by a drilling whelk (see page 13). Whelks eat shelled animals that are fixed to the rocks or are not very active. The whelk uses acid that softens the shell of its victim and then drills a neat hole with its tongue. It sticks its long snout through the hole and feasts on the soft living animal inside. Even the giant clam with its pair of thick, ridged shells is not safe. One giant clam shell 25cm long and 2cm thick was found with a hole drilled through it! The sundial shell by contrast selects easier prey and sucks the juices of soft zoanthid anemones.

These shells have been drilled and eaten by whelks – which are carnivorous snails with a coiled shell.

> **Things to do**
>
> ● Look carefully at the Venus ear shell on page 24 and find the row of holes where water flows out. Did you notice the hole in the centre, which was drilled by the whelk that ate the animal inside?
> ● See if you can find drilling whelks in action. Look among limpets, barnacles and mussels. Hold a whelk so that its foot touches a limpet or winkle that is covered with water and see what they both do.

Cone shells harpoon their prey

Some snails have venom that paralyses their prey. The cone shell has loose harpoon-shaped teeth that it jabs into its prey along with some venom. Be careful of cone shells: some of the larger species are fish eaters and are dangerous to humans as well. Others can give a sting like a bee. Most of the small common species, however, feed on marine worms and pose no threat to humans.

The **giant clam's** bright blue mantle contains tiny algae – plants that use sunlight to make food for themselves and the clam.

A **giant clam** into which a **branched murex whelk** is drilling a hole

Sundial shell feeding on zoanthids

A common **cone shell** paralysing a sea worm with its poisonous dart

Branched murex whelk

Rocky-shore intertidal life

Shellfish and their enemies

Molluscs have many enemies: oystercatchers jab shells off the rocks; seagulls drop mussels from a height to break them open; and octopuses, whelks and even spiny starfish all feed on them. However, their worst enemies are fish and crabs.

Protection

Some shells run and hide: top shells spin and flee from starfish and whelks, while angel wings can jet backwards by clapping their shells together. There is even a shell that can burrow into wood to find a safe hiding place. Oysters clamp shut so that they are safe inside their shell. You have to surprise a limpet if you want to knock it off a rock. It takes a force equal to lifting a 100kg weight to budge a large limpet once it has a firm grip. The false limpet is easy to pull off the rocks, but because its milky slime tastes awful, it is never eaten by birds or fish or drilled into by whelks.

Things to do

- Examine a variety of shells. How are they adapted to avoid being eaten?
- Find out where they come from and look around for likely enemies.

Many fish swallow shells whole

The rocksucker fish has a suction pad under its belly so that it can grip the rocks even in a strong current. Then it uses its two strong, curved teeth to prise limpets free. If, however, the shells have spines or knobbles, the fish finds them hard to swallow and will spit them up again.

Things to do

- Compare shells from different areas. Which ones are thicker? How long are their spines? How big are their openings? There are usually more predators in the warmer tropical waters on the east coast than in the colder waters on the west coast.
- Look at the tropical giant clam and the whelk on page 25 and see their thick, ridged shells.

The **false limpet** has unpleasant slime.

Plough shells burrow into the sand to escape.

Angel wings can swim by clapping their shells together to escape.

A **top shell** spins as it escapes from a whelk.

The **rocksucker fish** can swallow a **smooth rayed limpet** whole.

Fish can't easily swallow shells with spines.

Long-spined limpet

Spiny whelk

Spider shell

Girdled dogwhelk

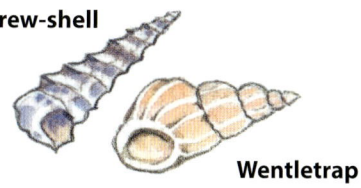
Screw-shell

Wentletrap

Shells that are strengthened by ridges

Crab attack

A thin shell that has a long, pointed spire and a wide mouth can easily be gripped and broken by a crab using its strong nippers. Animals with thicker shells are better protected – but must carry a heavier load with them. Many shells are ridged or knobbled to make them stronger without adding too much weight. Some shells also have a short spire and narrow opening to keep enemies out, or have a 'door' to close the opening against attackers.

The ridged nerita has a better chance than most of surviving attacks. Its shell is thick and ridged, with a flat spire. The opening has a strong, toothed lip. When the animal pulls itself back into its shell, it closes the entrance with a knobbly 'door'.

A **xanthid crab** breaking open a shell

Cowrie defence

Glossy cowries are a delight to any collector. These creatures have many amazing ways of avoiding a crab attack. The fleshy mantle of the cowrie can curve up and cover the top of the shell. The mantle has soft finger-like spines in mottled colours that blend in beautifully with seaweeds. It may also have an unpleasant acidic taste. The mantle covering keeps the shell very smooth and shiny. If the cowrie is in real danger it can pull back completely into its shell. The shell has no outer spire and the mouth is very narrow and strengthened with toothed lips. It would be as hard for a crab to break the polished cowrie shell open as for us to cut a glass marble in half with a pair of scissors. Live cowries are difficult to find because they hide in crevices, but they are not safe from the octopus, which can grip the shell with its suckers and bite a hole in it with its beak. Many different species of cowrie are found on the east coast of South Africa.

Marginella has a short spire and a narrow mouth to keep crabs out.

Shells with a short spire and narrow mouths or protective 'doors'

The **turban shell** or **alikreukel** reaches about 100mm in size by the time it is six years old.

Thick knobbly 'door'

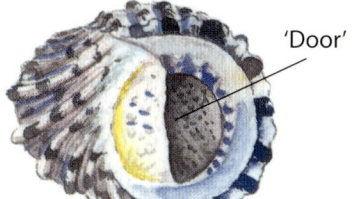
Ridged nerita
'Door'

Polished **cowrie shell** with narrow mouth and no spire

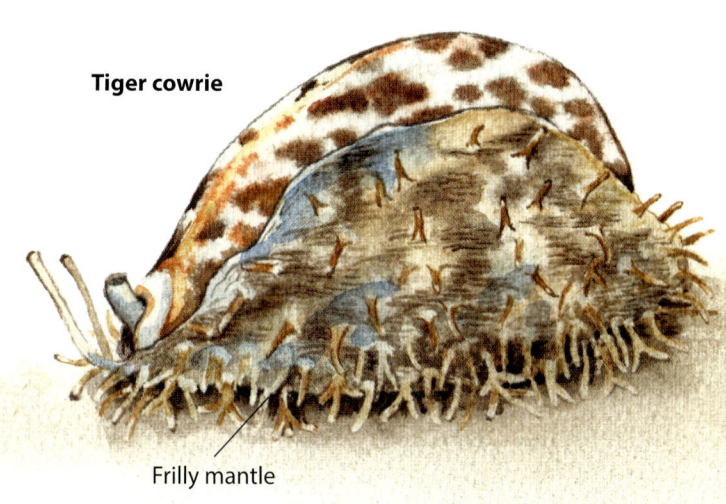
Tiger cowrie

Frilly mantle

Rocky-shore intertidal life

Rock lobsters and their relatives

Rock lobsters (often called crayfish) belong to the animal class called Crustacea, which includes crabs, prawns, shrimps, beach hoppers and even barnacles. Crustaceans are active creatures and have hard, jointed outer skeletons, two body regions, many legs and two pairs of feelers. When they get too big for their outer skeleton, they have to moult. Because they are tasty, crustaceans need extra protection to survive.

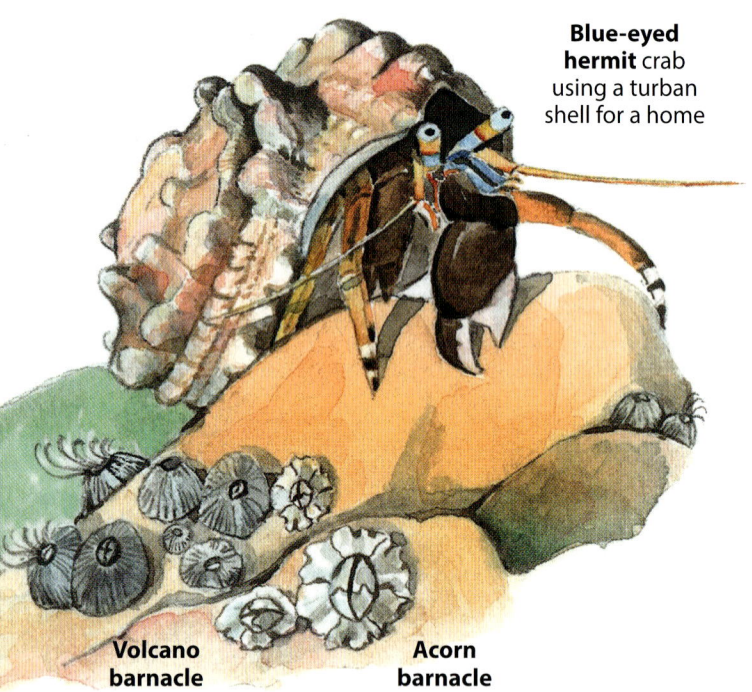

Blue-eyed hermit crab using a turban shell for a home

Volcano barnacle   **Acorn barnacle**

The hermit's house

The hermit crab uses a mollusc shell for a home. It can disappear into the shell and block the opening with a nipper. From time to time, as it grows, it has to move to a bigger shell. It feels carefully inside the new shell to make sure that it is empty and then, in a flash, transfers its soft tail from the old shell to the new one.

Things to do

- Place some empty shells near a hermit crab and see if it will move house.
- Examine a crustacean skeleton and see how the thin joints allow the parts to move.

Barnacles

Barnacles have changed so much to gain extra protection that they hardly look like crustaceans any more. They stand on their head inside a hard protective shell, and stick out only their fine, jointed legs to comb the water for food. Goose barnacles drift in the sea and have a long, flexible stalk that they use to attach themselves to anything that floats. Most acorn barnacles are cemented to the rocks, but some travel around the world attached to the hulls of ships or even to whales. These barnacles make the ship's hull rough, which slows its movement through the water. Ships have to be scraped and then painted with poisonous paint to stop new barnacle larvae from settling on them.

The **sponge crab** carries a protective cloak of sponge.

The **zebra shrimp** defends its territory against intruders. Why do you think it has stripes? Look on pages 50 and 51 for ideas.

Things to do

Look for goose barnacles on the beach after a storm. Place them in sea water so that you can watch them open and start to sweep the water with their legs.

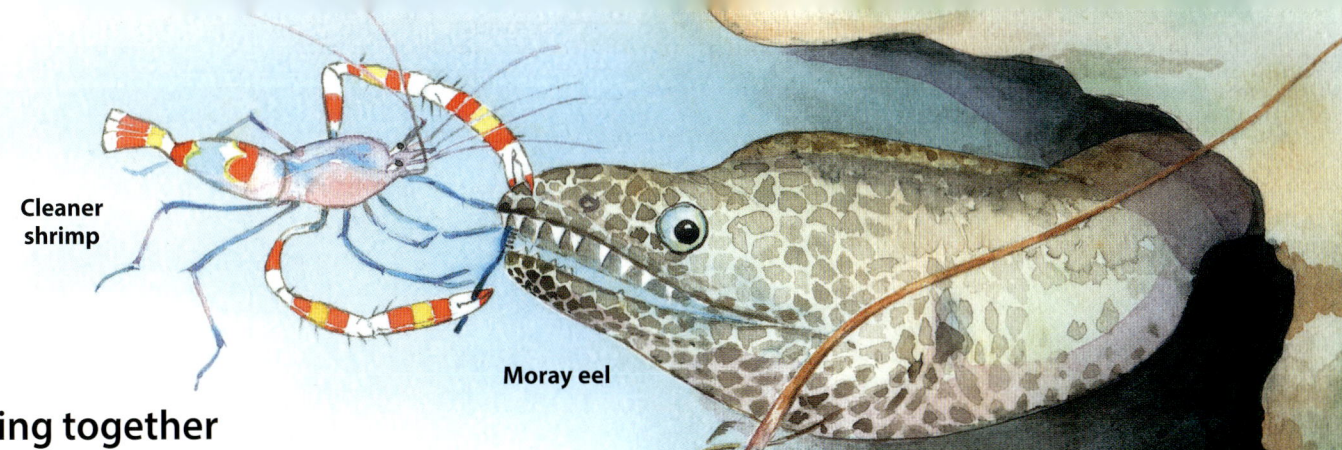

Cleaner shrimp

Moray eel

Living together

The dainty cleaner shrimp cleans the teeth and bodies of fish. Its bright colours remind fish not to eat this useful friend.

Snake-like moray eels often share their refuge with east coast rock lobsters. When an octopus feels along the ledges looking for a lobster meal, the moray dashes out and eats the octopus, both earning a meal and saving the lobster. Rock lobsters feed mainly on urchins, mussels and other shells.

The next time you eat a rock lobster, remember that is has moulted 13 times as a larva and is between 7 and 15 years old!

Prawns and shrimps

Swimming prawns and shrimps are active and often change colour to suit their surroundings (see sand shrimp, page 14). Sand prawns burrow in lagoons and estuaries. They help to make a healthy environment for burrowing creatures, as they turn over tons of sand while they sift for food, which helps to soften the sand and introduce oxygen. They are harvested as bait with special prawn pumps. This practice does a lot of damage, not only trampling and collapsing prawn burrows but also harming other burrowing animals.

East coast rock lobster (or crayfish)

Ribbed mussel

Papery burnupena

Did you know?

The papery burnupena whelk is not eaten by the west coast rock lobster. Its shell is encrusted with a bumpy red moss-animal colony, which is poisonous. In fact these whelks can eat rock lobsters!

Conservation

Are rock lobsters and prawns your favourite seafood? Many people rely on harvesting rock lobsters for their income. Rock lobsters are caught by divers or in baited traps. On a much larger scale, huge trawl nets are dragged along the seafloor to catch prawns. Sadly, many other animals are accidentally caught as bycatch and die as a result.

Fisheries researchers carefully assess the numbers of rock lobsters and calculate how many can be caught and how many must be left to reproduce for the future. It is important that everyone observes the regulations, because being greedy and poaching today can lead to poverty tomorrow, and rock lobster numbers are already very low.

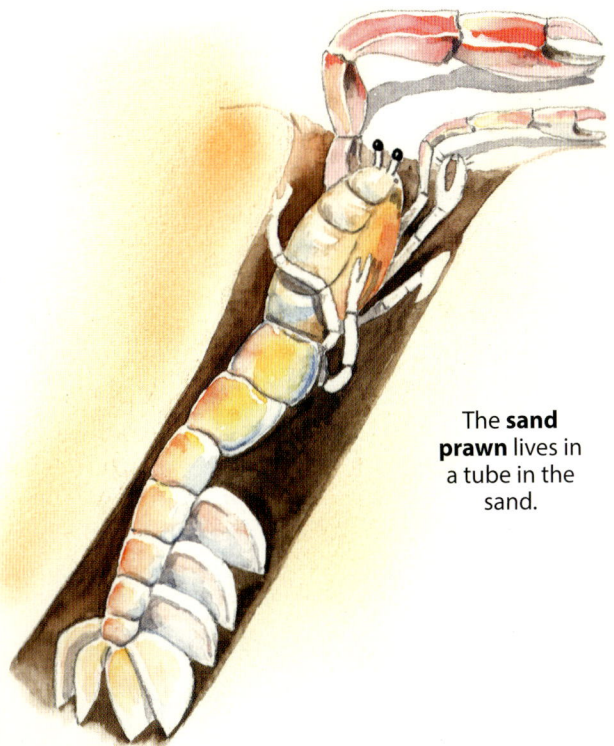

The **sand prawn** lives in a tube in the sand.

Rock pools and camouflage

Sit quietly and examine the edges of a rock pool. Drop bits of food into the water and shake the seaweeds. You'll be surprised how many little creatures emerge: most cannot survive out of water.

Hide and seek

Can you identify the following creatures in the picture below?

- The zebra fish has black and white stripes.
- A blacktail is a fish with a black spot on its tail.
- Strepies are common bait-fish that have yellow stripes.
- The young goat's-eye limpet matches the rock.
- The clown shrimp is only 1cm long. It grips the seaweed with its back legs and grabs food with its front legs, which are folded like those of a praying mantis.
- Two different types of sea lice, one pink and one green, look a bit like cockroaches. They can use their tails to swim.
- A goby is a fish with a blunt nose and large, delicate fins.
- The pipefish is long and thin.
- The shrimp-like amphipod has a humped body and can jump and swim.
- The seahorse grips seaweed with its tail.
- Blotcheye soldierfish are red with a black mark at the top of their eyes.
- The spiny seaweed crab hooks bits of seaweed onto its back to hide itself.
- Although the sea spider has eight legs, it is not a true spider.
- A pink flatworm has crept onto a rock. It can swim using its frilly body edges.
- A fan worm sticks out a feathery fan from its tube to collect food.
- The ragged scorpionfish has sharp poisonous spines on its back.
- The brittle-star has five spiny arms joined to a disc.

Things to do

- Float in a rock pool and look through a pair of goggles.
- Shake a bunch of seaweed in a jar of sea water. The creatures that dart out and swim around can be slowed down by placing them in a fridge for a while. Look at them with a magnifying lens.
- Look under boulders for hidden animals. Always replace the boulders as they were before.

Make a seaweed card

Seaweeds will stay fresh in a plastic bag for a few hours. Use thin seaweeds to make the most successful cards. Float the seaweed in a bowl of water. Slide a sheet of good drawing paper under the seaweed. Lift the paper carefully so that the seaweed settles on it. Cover the seaweed and card with a piece of cloth and press it between newspaper for a few days until dry. Peel the cloth off carefully. The seaweed will remain stuck to the paper by its own natural glue. Seaweeds' beautiful colours will last for years and they have a natural fungicide that prevents them from becoming mouldy. Marine biologists store their reference collections of seaweeds mounted on cards in this way.

Rock pools – living under water

Sea slugs

Sea slugs are molluscs (see page 13). They are soft-bodied animals related to snails. Although some sea slugs have an internal shell, and the beautiful bubble shell has a very thin shell, most adult sea slugs have no shell.

'Nude gills'

Sea slugs without shells are called nudibranchs, which means 'nude gills'. Their soft bodies have marvellous shapes and colours. Their gills often stick up like bright flexible fingers on their backs, or may look like a ring of feathers. Sea slugs have two feelers on the head with which they taste and smell. These creatures cannot survive out in the open on dry rocks – they always live under water and usually hide in seaweeds and sponges or under rocks.

A colourful warning

Most nudibranchs are unpleasant to eat because of poisonous chemicals in their skin. A fish has to take only the tiniest nibble to learn to leave these slugs alone in the future. Do not add them to a fish tank, as the fish might die. Other nudibranchs use 'second-hand' poisons. They feed on anemones or bluebottles that have stinging cells. The stings pass through the body and are stored in the slug's skin, ready to use against enemies (see page 37). Nudibranchs use bright colours to warn off predators.

The delicate bubble shell is unpleasant to eat.

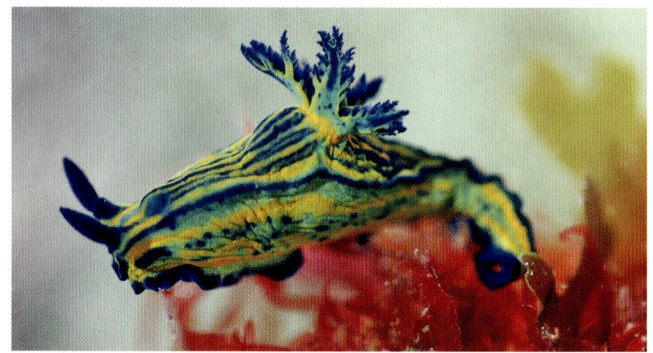
The colourful blue dragon nudibranch

The toxins of the warty nudibranch can kill fish.

Things to do

- At low tide, look among seaweeds and under rocks for nudibranchs. They are often small, but there are many different types. Watch what other animals do when they meet a sea slug.
- Place them in a pool or jar where you can appreciate their beauty. Remember to carefully replace the rocks and nudibranchs as you found them.

This bright sea slug eats sponges and sea anemones.

A hooded nudibranch creeping up to catch an isopod

A black nudibranch on a grey moss animal

The sea hare lays strings of eggs that look like spaghetti.

The black nudibranch lays a yellow ribbon of eggs.

Camouflage for survival

Some sea slugs have wonderful camouflage. Those that live in sandy lagoons are spotted and sandy in colour. They give off a nasty purple dye if disturbed. Their eggs look like a tangle of yellow string. The sea hare *Aplysia* has a thin internal shell. The blue sea swallow, *Glaucus* (see page 7), floats on the ocean. It is blue on top and blends with the sea when viewed from above. Underneath it is silver, so from a fish's point of view it is also invisible.

Things to do

Look in tidal swimming pools and lagoons for sea hares. Often you will spot their spaghetti-like eggs before you notice the big soft slugs.

Crowned nudibranch

Spanish dancers are among a few nudibranchs that can swim.

This **nudibranch** has feathery gills.

Rock pools – living under water

Anemones and corals

The anemones and their relatives – corals, sea fans and hydroids – all have stinging cells and belong to the group Cnidaria, which means 'nettle'. They are also related to jellyfish and bluebottles (see pages 6 and 7).

Anemones are animals

Sea anemones look like beautiful soft flowers, but they are in fact animals. If a crushed shell or a small animal lands in an anemone, it is grabbed by the sticky tentacles and pulled into the anemone's mouth. The tentacles are covered with microscopic stinging cells. Each cell is like a little sac with a tail coiled inside. The tail can shoot out to entangle prey while also delivering an injection of paralysing venom. The anemone also uses it stings to protect itself. The stings of most anemones can't penetrate human skin, so they are generally not harmful to us.

Colourful sandy anemones live in dense colonies.

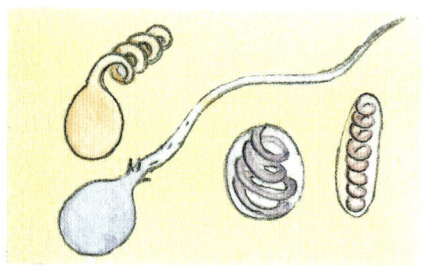
Stinging cells as seen through a microscope

Things to do

- Feed an anemone. Place your finger on the tentacles and feel them grab you.
- If your school or someone you know has a microscope, ask if you can use it to view an anemone's stinging cells. This is done by touching the tentacles with a microscope slide. First licking the slide helps to gather more stinging cells. This is because the stings are released in response to both touch and taste.

Some anemones even attack other anemones that creep into their feeding space. The orange anemone is one of these. The base of each tentacle is packed with stinging cells and swells up to sting the intruder. Sandy anemones, by contrast, live closely packed together; the zoanthids on the east coast are even joined together in huge sheets (see page 19).

Corals

Corals have many different shapes. Coral colonies may look like rocks or plants, but they are really groups of animals. Colonies of hard corals are supported by skeletons of lime (calcium carbonate) and form coral reefs. The surface of coral has lots of little cups. Each cup contains a small anemone-like polyp, with tentacles and a mouth leading to a stomach.

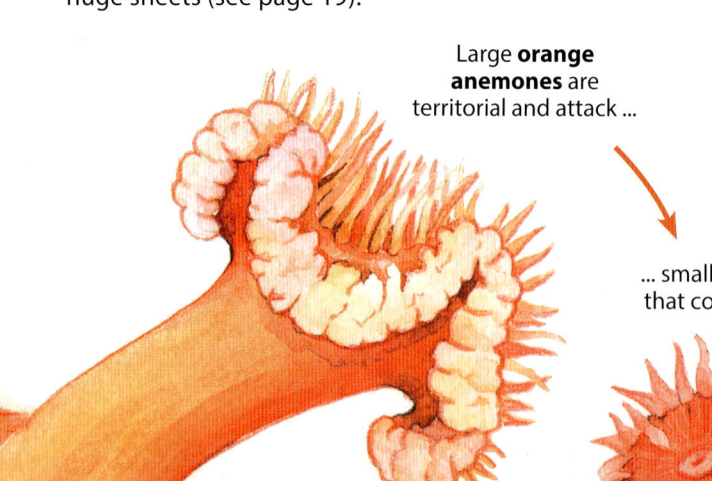
Large **orange anemones** are territorial and attack …
… smaller **anemones** that come too close.

Green zoanthids
Sandy zoanthids

Two types of delicate feather hydroids

The polyps of soft corals have eight feathery tentacles.

Detail of a red sea fan with white polyps

A novel food supply – symbiosis

It is difficult for crowded polyps and zoanthids to catch enough food to survive. They have tiny green plants, called algae, living in their bodies. These algae use the waste carbon dioxide and nitrogen from the corals to make food, which they share with their coral host. They also help to build the corals' beautiful skeletons. This is an example of symbiosis, where a plant and an animal live together, to the benefit of both.

Feather hydroids

Delicate feather hydroids are made up of many tiny feeding polyps growing on a fern-like stalk. The hydroid can reproduce and spread by budding off little jellyfish-like medusa that float away, produce eggs and start a new colony.

Sea fans and soft corals

The little creatures (polyps) that make up sea fans and soft corals are different from anemones: they have eight feathery tentacles. Soft corals are delicate and they sway gently in the water. They come in many beautiful colours. Red sea fans have red stems and can form underwater forests 3m tall. When they get this big, they must be extremely old, because red sea fans grow only a few millimetres a year.

Don't be be tempted to collect (or buy) sea fans and corals – they are much more attractive when alive.

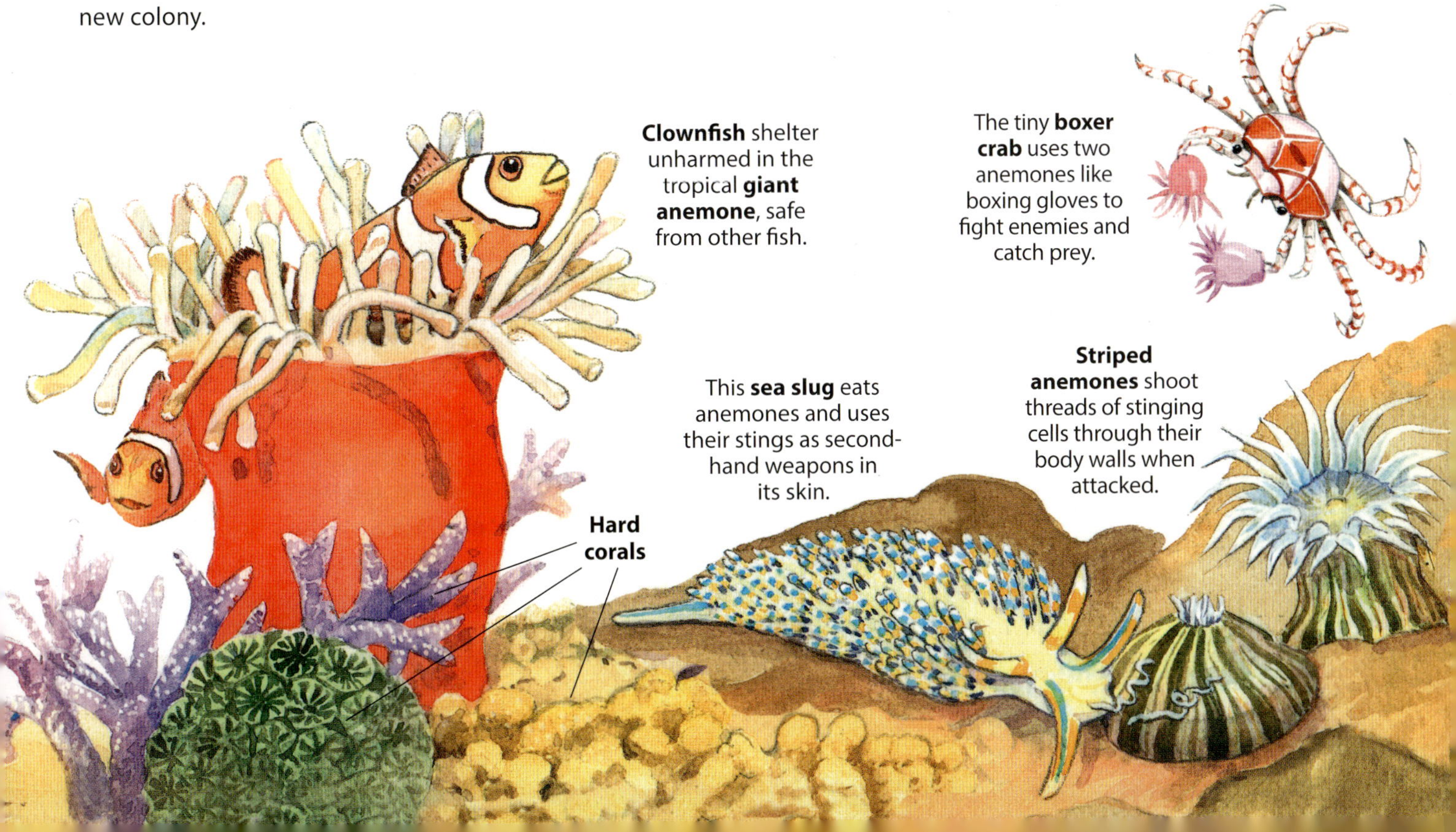

Clownfish shelter unharmed in the tropical **giant anemone**, safe from other fish.

The tiny **boxer crab** uses two anemones like boxing gloves to fight enemies and catch prey.

This **sea slug** eats anemones and uses their stings as second-hand weapons in its skin.

Striped anemones shoot threads of stinging cells through their body walls when attacked.

Hard corals

Rock pools – living under water

The sea stars

Starfish, brittle-stars and feather stars have no head, no front and no back – it is hard to believe that they are living creatures. But they are fascinating animals, full of surprises. They cannot live out of water, so search for them in rock pools.

Starfish have spiny skins

Starfish have spiny skin that is hard but can bend. If you look at it through a magnifying glass you will see a mosaic of knobbly plates. These plates are held together by elastic threads. The spiny skin grows as the starfish gets bigger and so, unlike crabs, starfish do not have to moult. Seaweeds and barnacles do not grow on starfish, because the skin covering the plates is dotted with tiny pincer-like nippers that remove anything that tries to settle on it.

Red starfish

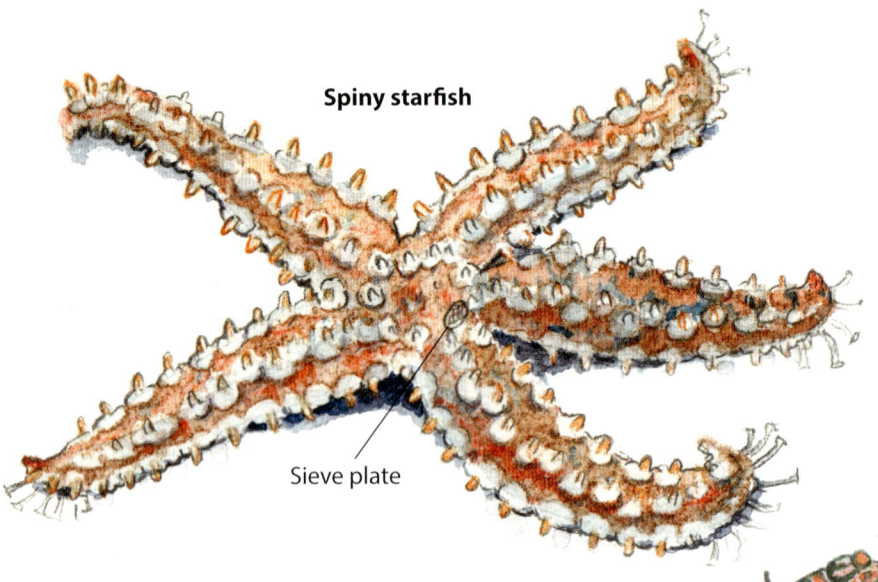

Spiny starfish

Sieve plate

A spiny carnivore

Most southern African starfish feed on fine plant material, but the large spiny starfish is a carnivore. It feeds on redbait and molluscs. It humps over a mussel and pulls the two halves of the shell apart with its tube feet. As one set of tube feet tire, so another team takes over until the poor mussel can't keep its shell closed any longer. The starfish then sticks its stomach inside the shell and eats the animal.

Things to do

Place a large spiny starfish so that it touches a winkle or a limpet in a pool. What do they do? Notice the red sense organ at the tip of each of the starfish's arms.

The tube feet of the starfish end in suckers that grip rocks. Simple tubes on top act as gills.

Creeping on tube feet

Starfish usually have five arms, beneath which are rows of wriggling tube feet with suckers at their tips. These grip the rocks and can move the starfish in any direction. Instead of blood, starfish have sea water running through tubes in their bodies. These tubes are joined to the tube feet, which can be lengthened by having water pumped into them. Sea water enters the tube system through a sieve plate on the top of the starfish. Starfish can regrow arms that are lost.

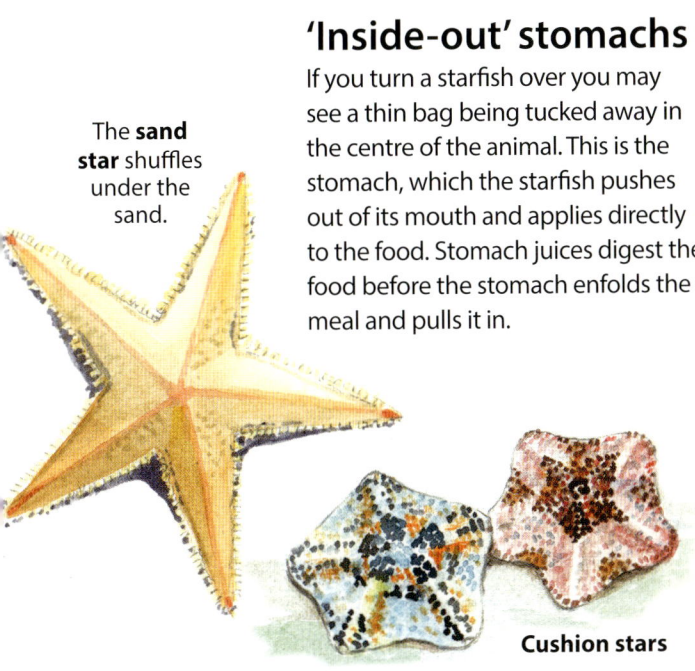

The **sand star** shuffles under the sand.

'Inside-out' stomachs

If you turn a starfish over you may see a thin bag being tucked away in the centre of the animal. This is the stomach, which the starfish pushes out of its mouth and applies directly to the food. Stomach juices digest the food before the stomach enfolds the meal and pulls it in.

Cushion stars

A **basket-star** on a red sea fan

The branched arms capture food.

Things to do

- The short-armed cushion star has amazing camouflage. Search in rock pools for different coloured cushion stars. How well do they match the rocks on which you find them?
- Turn a starfish over and look for its stomach. Watch the tube feet in action and feel them suck on your hand. Be very careful not to damage the tube feet.

Feather stars

Divers often find feather stars. These stars grip rocks with the short, hooked arms beneath their bodies and have 10 or more long feathery arms that they use to collect fine bits of food. Some 350 million years ago the ancestors of today's feather stars were among the most common of sea creatures.

Brittle-stars

Brittle-stars have long, delicate arms joined to a disc in the centre. They are called 'brittle-stars' because their arms break off easily. Some brittle-stars are smooth and scaly, but others have many spines. They often hide under boulders and their long arms can be seen sticking out of crevices to catch bits of food in the water. The most spectacular brittle-stars are the black-and-white-patterned basket-stars. The arms of these big brittle-stars have many branches with beautifully curled tips. Most starfish and brittle-stars lay eggs that hatch into swimming larvae, but in some species the young grow in pouches inside their mothers.

Feather stars don't have tube feet like other sea-stars.

The brittle-star moves by writhing its arms. Its tube feet do not have suckers.

Rock pools – living under water

Urchins and sea cucumbers

Sea urchins and sea cucumbers are related to starfish, although they look very different. They are all part of a group of animals called the echinoderms, which means 'spiny skins' or 'hedgehogs'.

Prickly balls

Live sea urchins are rounded and prickly. They can control their spines and use them for protection, walking and even digging. They can also walk with the rows of tube feet between their spines. These feet can grip pieces of shell or seaweed for use as a sunshield or for camouflage. Among their spines and tube feet, urchins also have stalked nippers with tiny jaws, which are used to keep the skin clean and to attack predators. For eating, sea urchins have more complex jaws with five strong teeth. They eat seaweeds and scrape young seaweeds from the rocks. One species, the Cape sea urchin, provides a prickly hideout where baby abalone can shelter from predators. When the urchins trap pieces of kelp for food, the young abalone gain an easy feast. If rock lobsters eat too many urchins in an area, then the baby abalone there lose their hidey-holes and numbers decline.

The Cape sea urchin's solid spines are not venomous.

Urchin shells

Urchin shells, or sea pumpkins, are often found lying on the shore. The shell is like a jigsaw puzzle of plates joined together. It has rows of small holes through which the tube feet once protruded, and knobs to which the spines were attached. The anus is at the centre of the shell. One of the plates forms a sieve through which water would have flowed to pump up the tube feet. An urchin does not have to moult, as its shell grows with it.

The sea pumpkin is the shell of a dead sea urchin.

Detail of a Cape sea urchin shell showing the central anus, five holes where the eggs are released and the triangular sieve plate.

Watch sea urchins wave their spines and tube feet. Use a magnifying glass to look for the tiny stalked nippers with three jaws (see arrow).

Pansy shell

A pansy shell is actually the skeleton of a burrowing sea urchin. The flower-like pattern of holes is where the live urchin's gills would stick out. The living urchin uses short spines to dig itself into the sand, where it feeds on fine food particles.

The delicate pansy shell is the skeleton of a type of burrowing sea urchin.

Sea cucumbers

Sea cucumbers usually lie under rocks or are partly buried in the sand on the ocean floor. They look like tough-skinned sausages. Some are black, but many are red, yellow, purple or pink. They collect food with the branched tentacles that stick out of the mouth. If they are disturbed, some cucumbers squirt out sticky threads that entangle their enemies. Others will spit out their whole gut as an offering to a fish so that they can escape. They grow a new gut in its place.

Needle urchins are dangerous

The needle urchin has long, hollow spines. Be careful not to stand or sit on this 'pincushion', because the spine tips break off releasing venom, and cannot easily be pulled out, as they are covered with tiny hooks. They can be dissolved with vinegar or dug out with a needle. If, however, they have penetrated deeply, you may need the help of a doctor.

Things to do

Find a sea cucumber and watch until it expands its tentacles and starts feeding.

The black needle urchin on the east coast has long, hollow, venomous spines that point towards any danger.

A **sea cucumber's** sticky threads entangling a predatory **long-nosed butterflyfish**

Branched tentacles for collecting food

Rock pools – living under water

Danger

There aren't many dangerous animals on southern Africa's seashores. Even so, you should take a careful look at the animals on this page, as these can pose some danger. Make sure that you are able to recognize them – especially the stonefish. Beware of animals that have spines, and remember that bright colours often warn that the creature is dangerous. (See also bluebottles, box jellyfish, needle urchins and sharks, pages 6, 7, 39 and 52).

The fireworm and the red and purple sponges shown here have irritant spines.

Sponges

Sponges are simple animals that form colonies. They sieve food from the water as it passes through their porous body. They are often poisonous and brightly coloured. Some have tiny glassy needles that can cause a skin rash if you touch such a sponge. Look out for the crafty sponge crab that grows a piece of sponge on its back for protection and camouflage (see page 28).

The fireworm

The fireworm has stiff bristles along its body. These help the worm to grip as it wriggles along. They also give a painful sting if the worm is disturbed. These worms are found on the east coast.

Sea snake

The sea snake uses its flat black-and-yellow tail like a flipper for swimming. It cannot move on land. Luckily, it is slow to attack but, if you do see one in the water, remember that it is a dangerously venomous snake.

Treatment

Worm bristles and sponge spines can be removed with tweezers or covered with a plaster for a day or two until they work their way out.

An ordinary snakebite kit will not be effective against the bite of a sea snake. Get medical help. Bandage the limb right up into the armpit or groin to prevent the venom being carried quickly through the lymph system. Notify the hospital of the type of snake involved.

The **sea snake** uses its flat tail for swimming.

The **devil firefish** or **lionfish** occurs in warm water.

Devil firefish

You will be enchanted if you find a devil firefish. It is sometimes called a lionfish, because its fins fan out like the mane of a lion. However, its bright stripes and long fins are a warning to all to keep their distance, for along the back of this fish is a row of sharp, venomous spines. The lionfish uses its long fins to herd shrimps and fish into a corner so that it is easy to catch them.

Pufferfish

Poisonous puffer

The *blaasop* or pufferfish can blow itself up. It is often washed up on the beach or hooked by anglers. If the flesh of the pufferfish is eaten, it is poisonous enough to kill a person. Occasionally its spiny relative the porcupinefish, which is also poisonous, can be found (see page 62).

Why are there more dangerous creatures in tropical waters than in cooler waters? (Clue: less food is available in warmer waters. See pages 58–59.)

Treatment

All venomous stings, from those of bluebottles (see page 6) to stonefish, can be treated by soaking the wound in very hot water. This breaks down the venom and draws it out of the wound.

When there is an allergic reaction to a sting, an antihistamine can be used.

If you are bitten or badly stung by a dangerous animal, see a doctor at once.

Deadly stonefish

The stonefish is the most venomous fish of all. Not only does it contain deadly venom in the sharp spines along its back, but its camouflage is almost perfect. Even when you know where the fish is, it is still hard to spot. The stonefish lives in the warm waters of northern KwaZulu-Natal and in coral reefs. It is important to wear shoes when you paddle on a coral reef and it is a good idea to have a stick to poke the area ahead of you before you take each step.

Deadly **stonefish**

Venomous spines

Diving deeper

The kelp forest

Magnificent underwater forests grow along the west coast of South Africa. The 'trees' in these forests are large brown seaweeds known as kelp and can be up to 12m tall. They break the force of the waves and provide shelter and food for a community of seaweeds and animals.

A forest reaching for light

Tall kelps form a shady canopy. Fine branching seaweeds grow on them, like ferns and creepers that sway in the waves. Bushy seaweeds make up the understorey plants. On the ocean bed, where there is little wave movement, flat red seaweeds spread out to capture the scarce blue light that filters through the watery forest.

Giants and midgets

Kelps shed millions of spores, each smaller than a pinprick. They grow into tiny male and female plants and look like a brown scum on the rocks. Fertilized eggs from these midget plants grow into giant kelps.

Things to do

A tasty pudding can be made by boiling 1 cup of red ribbons seaweed in 2 cups of water for about 20 minutes to extract the jelly (called agar). Then remove the seaweed, add sugar and flavourings to the liquid, and allow it to set in the fridge. Getting the right seaweed is important, though, as some species are poisonous!

Red ribbons

Split-fan kelp

Did you know?

- Crops grow three times better when liquidized kelp is added to the fertilizer.
- Kelp is used in toothpaste, ice cream and many other products.

Kelps are food factories

Like other plants, kelps can make simple sugars from water and the gas carbon dioxide. To do this, they depend on the energy of sunlight, which is absorbed by green chlorophyll pigments in their cells (see page 22). Green seaweeds grow only in shallow water because chlorophyll cannot absorb the blue light you get in deeper water. Brown and red seaweeds have additional pigments that can absorb the blue light and pass this energy to their chlorophyll, so they can grow at the surface and at greater depths.

A vast food supply

Kelps grow very quickly, but the waves constantly wear down the tips of their leaf-like blades. Each blade grows like a conveyor belt, from its base and not its tip, and, in this way, is replaced up to six times per year.

Some animals – perlemoen (abalone), limpets, sea urchins, sea lice and strepies – feed directly on kelp by scraping at the fronds and sporelings, or trapping drift kelp. But many more filter tiny bits of kelp from the water. Mussels, redbait, sea cucumbers and sponges feed on the fine kelp soup supplied when the tips of the fronds are worn away. In turn, these animals become a feast for predators like rock lobsters, octopuses, seals and fish.

Why do you think some kelps have air bladders?

Sea bamboo

Kelp limpet

Air bladder

Bladder kelp

Things to do

Examine kelp plants stranded on the beach.
- Look for scrape marks where snails or sea lice have been grazing.
- Feel the raised patches on the blades where spores are produced.
- Look for the branching, root-like 'holdfast' that the seaweed uses to grip the rocky seafloor. How many seaweeds, worms and shells are living on this 'anchor'?

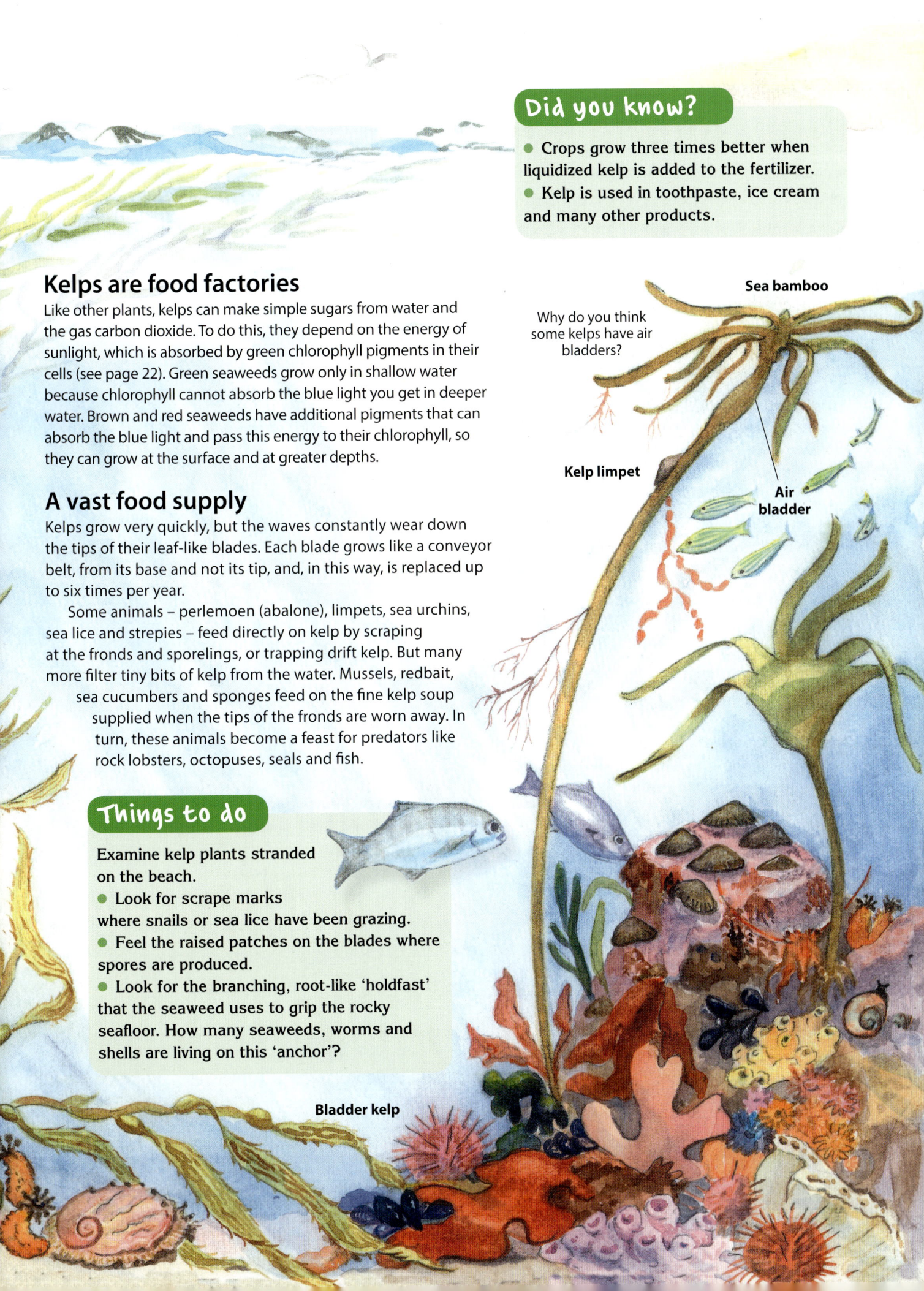

Diving deeper

Plankton and red tides

A food chain (like the one on page 15) shows the order in which different organisms feed on each other. Plants are always the first link in a food chain, because they can produce their own food from sunlight and don't need to consume other organisms. In deep water, where seaweeds don't grow, the main plant life consists of tiny algae called phytoplankton. Many animals depend on this algae for food, but sometimes an oversupply or 'red tide' occurs, which can be toxic to some creatures.

Plankton – tiny, floating plants or animals

Floating in the sea, among the phytoplankton, we also find a variety of minute animals that feed on it, called zooplankton. Collectively, these tiny plants and animals are known as plankton. It can be difficult to decide whether plankton cells are animals or plants, because they can move: if you look at plankton under a microscope you'll see tiny cells spinning along, driven by hair-like tails.

Scientists describe plants (like phytoplankton) as primary *producers* because they produce their own food. Animals, like zooplankton, that eat plants are primary *consumers* because they consume the primary producers. Animals that eat these primary consumers are called secondary consumers, and form the next link in the food chain.

Filter feeders

Many creatures are adapted to sieve plankton from the sea for food. They range from small zooplankton to larger mussels, sponges and sardines, and even include manta rays and huge whales. Filter feeders usually collect plankton using fine hairs, feathery tentacles or their gills.

Water enters the mouth of a **sardine** and comb-like 'gill rakers' sieve plankton from the water, as it flows out between the gills.

Sardines (pilchards) are a good example of secondary consumers. They eat zooplankton.

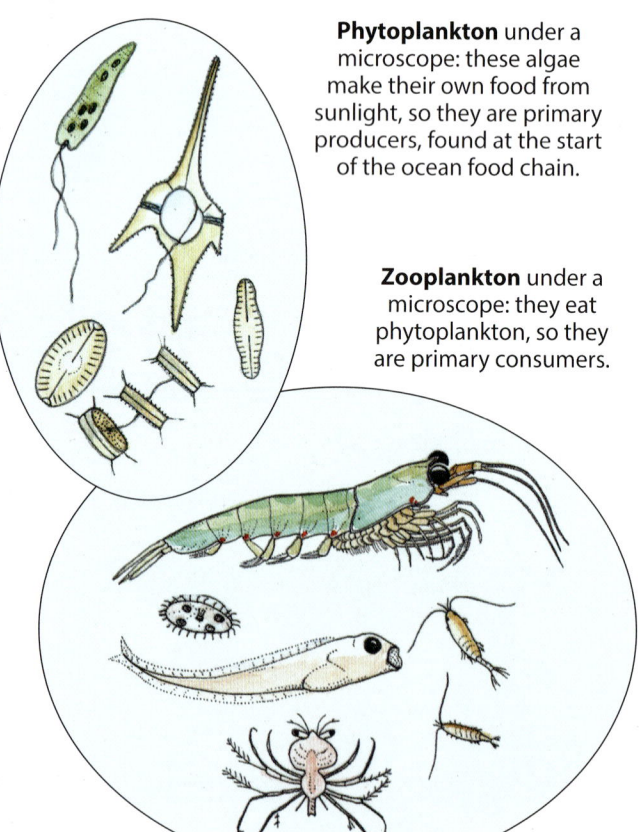

Phytoplankton under a microscope: these algae make their own food from sunlight, so they are primary producers, found at the start of the ocean food chain.

Zooplankton under a microscope: they eat phytoplankton, so they are primary consumers.

Things to do

Break open the two halves of a mussel shell. You will see the 'beard' that glues the shell to the rock, and the strong muscle that holds the shell halves closed. The soft body of the animal is yellow, orange, red or brown depending on the type of mussel and whether it is male or female. The two folded, frilly flaps below the body are the gills, which are used for breathing and feeding. The gills also have fine hairs for collecting food from the water and moving it to the mouth.

Brown mussel cut open

Muscle · Gill · Beard · Foot

What is red tide?

Sometimes the phytoplankton multiplies very quickly and forms a red or brown scum floating on the water. This is called a red tide. Some types of red tide flash with phosphorescent light at night. Others can be poisonous, and when filter feeders such as mussels and oysters feed on them, the poisons are concentrated and stored in their bodies for several months. If you eat these mussels they may be toxic enough to kill you. That is why the Department of Agriculture, Forestry and Fisheries (DAFF) usually issues a warning if a red tide has been seen. Animals like rock lobsters are not filter feeders and do not become poisonous from red tide. Birds and most marine animals are not harmed by red tide unless they eat poisoned shellfish.

Oxygen shortages

If the red tide is very thick, and there is no wind to blow it offshore, it will die and sink to the seafloor and start to rot. Bacteria that cause decay can use up all the oxygen in the water. As a result, bottom-dwelling fish and rock lobsters will start suffocating. They then move to the water surface or, in the case of lobsters, walk out of the sea, in search of oxygen, but may become stranded and die.

The great lobster walk-out

In 1997 a red tide occurred near Elands Bay on the west coast, and about 10 million rock lobsters walked out and were stranded on the rocks. They weighed about 2,000 tons, which is as much as an entire year's catch for the lobster industry. Around 500 tons were rescued and returned to the sea elsewhere, but the rest died. Many of the rock lobsters were small, and it took years for the population to recover.

Rock lobster (crayfish)

Rescuing rock lobsters stranded at Elands Bay. Were these lobsters poisonous?

Diving deeper

Fish and fisheries

Most people think of fish in terms of either catching or eating them. When you next eat a fish, take a good look at its shape, fins and armour of overlapping scales. If you can catch one, feel how smooth and slippery the skin is.

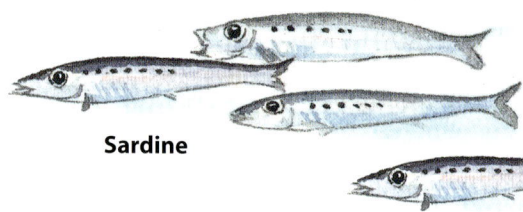
Sardine

A fisherman throws his impressive haul of snoek ashore.

Fish shapes and fins
Fast-swimming fish are torpedo-shaped and use their powerful tails to swim. Pairs of fins, on the sides and belly, act like oars and help them to turn and stop. Fish that swim in and out of caves and reefs usually have larger side-fins for steering.

Senses
Along the side of a fish's body there is a sense organ called the 'lateral line'. This organ detects vibrations in the water and helps the fish to navigate – even in the dark. Sound travels easily through water, and fish have internal ears for hearing, located just behind their eyes. Inside the fish there is also an organ called the 'swim bladder,' which is filled with gas to stop the fish from sinking. Sometimes this bladder acts like a drum, amplifying sounds and passing them to the internal ears. Fish do not need eyelids or lashes, as their eyes are washed and kept clean by the sea.

Did you know?
To help them balance, fish have a small, pebble-like bone that rests on a sensitive pad in each ear. Scientists can cut slices through these bones and then count the growth rings to work out the age of a fish. This is rather like counting the rings on a tree trunk. Look out for the ear bones in a cooked fish head.

In river mouths (estuaries) the water is less salty and only certain fish can live there, such as those illustrated below.

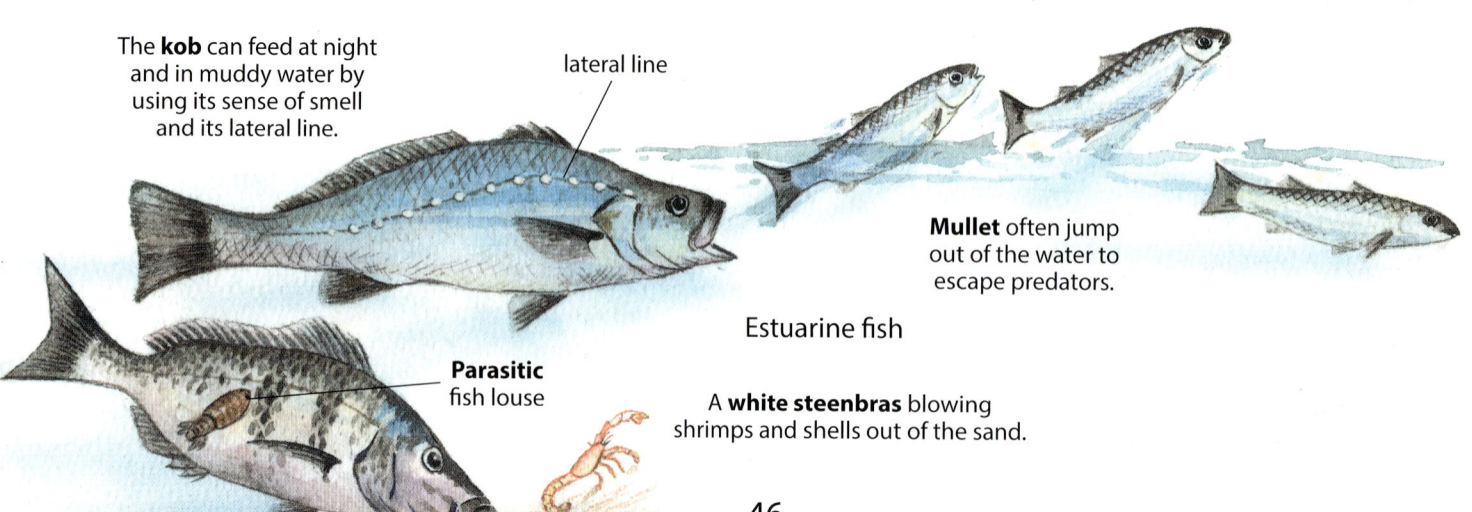

The **kob** can feed at night and in muddy water by using its sense of smell and its lateral line.

lateral line

Mullet often jump out of the water to escape predators.

Estuarine fish

Parasitic fish louse

A **white steenbras** blowing shrimps and shells out of the sand.

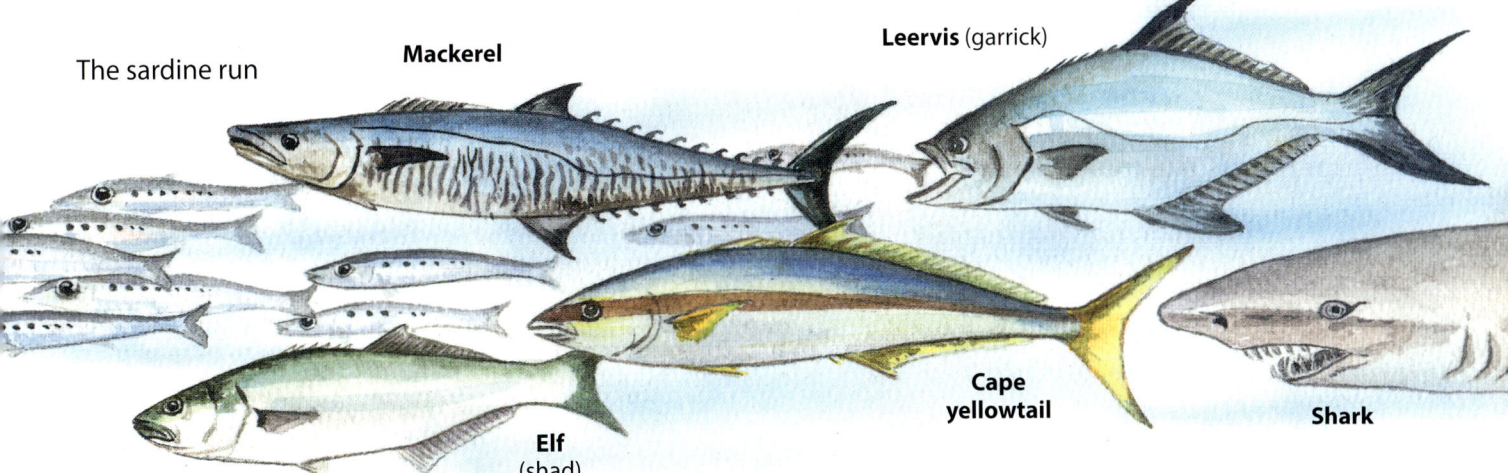

The sardine run

Mackerel

Leervis (garrick)

Elf (shad)

Cape yellowtail

Shark

The sardine run: sardines migrate up the east coast in winter and are followed by hunting fish, dolphins, whales and birds.

Safety in numbers

Fish that swim in the open ocean have nowhere to hide. It is safer for them to swim in schools, because predators are confused by the movement of all the fish at once and find it hard to decide which one to catch. A fish also uses less energy when it swims in the slipstream of the fish ahead. However, schools of fish are not safe from harvesting, because they are large enough to be spotted from aeroplanes or located with echo-sounders. The fishing boats then encircle the fish with a large net, and the whole shimmering school is dragged on board.

It is very important that humans don't catch so many fish that there are not enough left to breed. In southern Africa, fisheries departments have to decide on the maximum quantity of fish that individuals or businesses may harvest each year. Small or endangered fish species must be returned to the sea alive.

Did you know?

To learn more about fish populations, scientists and anglers catch fish, measure them, attach harmless numbered tags to them, and release them back into the ocean. If you catch a tagged fish, you should note its identification number, measure the fish, release it alive, and notify the authorities using the phone number or website on the tag. They can tell you when and where the fish was tagged and how much it has grown.

Things to do

Examine a fish:
- Look at the scales and find the lateral line. Cut open the gut and see what the fish has been eating.
- Study the gills. They are red from the blood that flows through them to collect oxygen from the water. Filter feeders have gill rakers that look like combs. They net bits of food from the water as it flows between the gills. Sardines, for example, have 100 gill rakers on each gill (see page 44).
- Boil the fish's head and clean and bleach all the strangely shaped bones. Paste them onto coloured paper to make attractive pictures or try to reconstruct the fish's head.

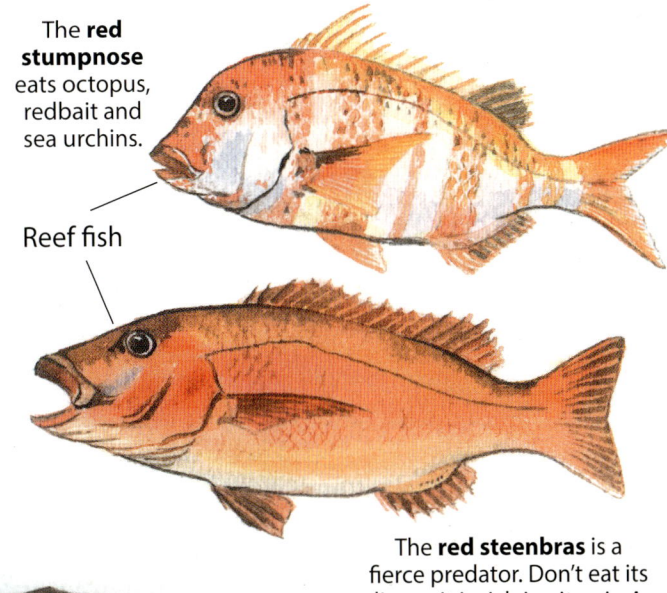

The **red stumpnose** eats octopus, redbait and sea urchins.

Reef fish

The **red steenbras** is a fierce predator. Don't eat its liver – it is rich in vitamin A and can be poisonous.

Sole

Bottom dwellers are flattened and a mottled brown colour.

Kingklip

Diving deeper

Strange and important fish

An amazing variety of fish swim in the sea. Some fish are of interest because of their ancient origins, which show us what the earliest fish were like. Others give us an idea of the link between fish and land vertebrates, such as frogs and reptiles. Some are adapted to live in surface waters, while others are best suited to life at great depths.

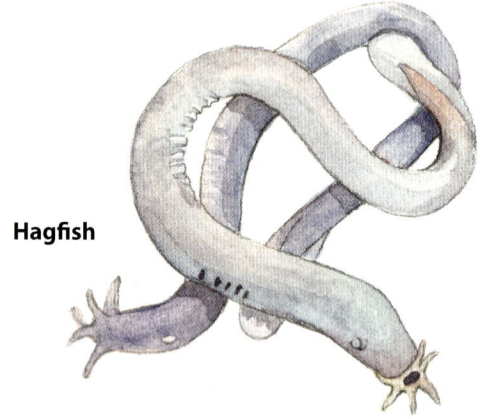

Hagfish

Hagfish – ancient origins

Hagfish are primitive fish, with jawless mouths and no fins or scales, and are thought to resemble the very earliest known fish. They use sensory whiskers to feel their way, because their eyes are poorly developed and lie under their skin. Many people fear them because they look like snakes, but they are harmless. Anglers hate them because they are often caught on fishing lines and produce foul slime for defence. Other fish will not come near bait with hagfish slime on it.

Coelacanth – an important find

In 1938 a strange 2-metre-long fish was caught off South Africa. This was hailed as the discovery of the century, because this fish was thought to have been extinct for about 70 million years and was known only from fossils. Marjory Courtney-Latimer made this exciting discovery, and Professor JLB Smith confirmed that it was a coelacanth. Fishermen on the Comoro Islands off East Africa had also unknowingly caught the occasional coelacanth but would throw them back because they were not good to eat. Scientists believe that the first vertebrates to live on land, some 350 million years ago, were creatures rather like coelacanths, which could use their stout fins for walking.

Mudhoppers

Mudhoppers are little fish that crawl out of the water and hop over the mud of mangrove swamps. Like the coelacanth, they have leg-like fins. They can survive out of water for some time because they store water in their gill chambers. They look a bit like tadpoles.

Mudhoppers

Did you know?

In the year 2000, divers found about 30 live coelacanths in deep canyons near Sodwana. These coelacanths are protected in iSimangaliso Wetland Park.

Coelacanths often swim head down using electric pulses to test the seafloor for food.

Eggs the size of oranges develop inside the female until the young are ready to be born.

A male **seahorse** squeezing many miniature babies out of his pouch

Seahorses

Seahorses are perhaps the most endearing of little fish. They drift through eelgrass in lagoons, relying on camouflage for protection. Interestingly, it is the male who incubates the babies. The female lays her eggs in a pouch on the male's belly, where they hatch and grow. Eventually the babies pop out and drift away. Seahorses have an armour of fused scales. They are endangered because people collect them for curios and home aquaria.

Sunfish at the surface

The sunfish basks in surface waters, slurping up jellyfish. This weird flat fish is the largest of the bony fish, weighs up to 1,000 kilograms and produces 300 million eggs. It is an intelligent, recently evolved fish. Its tail is reduced to a short rudder used for steering, while the large fins paddle it along. Its leathery skin has no scales.

Sunfish get their name from their habit of floating at the water surface, soaking up sunshine.

A **shrimpfish** is almost invisible as it swims, head down, feeding on plankton.

Things to do

Visit an aquarium or museum to see some of these strange fish. How many different kinds can you see in one visit?

Lantern fish can light up

Many deep-water fish have organs called photophores that produce flashing lights. These are used to find prey, confuse predators and assist in finding mates. Lantern fish have many small lights. There are millions of lantern fish in South African waters, and humans can eat them, although they are not as good as pilchards and anchovies. Fishermen should not net too many of them, though, as they are an important food for snoek, yellowtail, hake and squid.

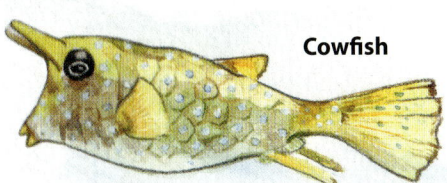

Cowfish

Lantern fish

Diving deeper

Tropical fish – an explosion of colour

Vivid fish with exotic patterns dart among the colourful corals and sponges found on the warm tropical reefs of the east coast. The fish are brightest when they are active: the strikingly coloured black-and-white clown triggerfish, for instance, fades to pale grey when it sleeps.

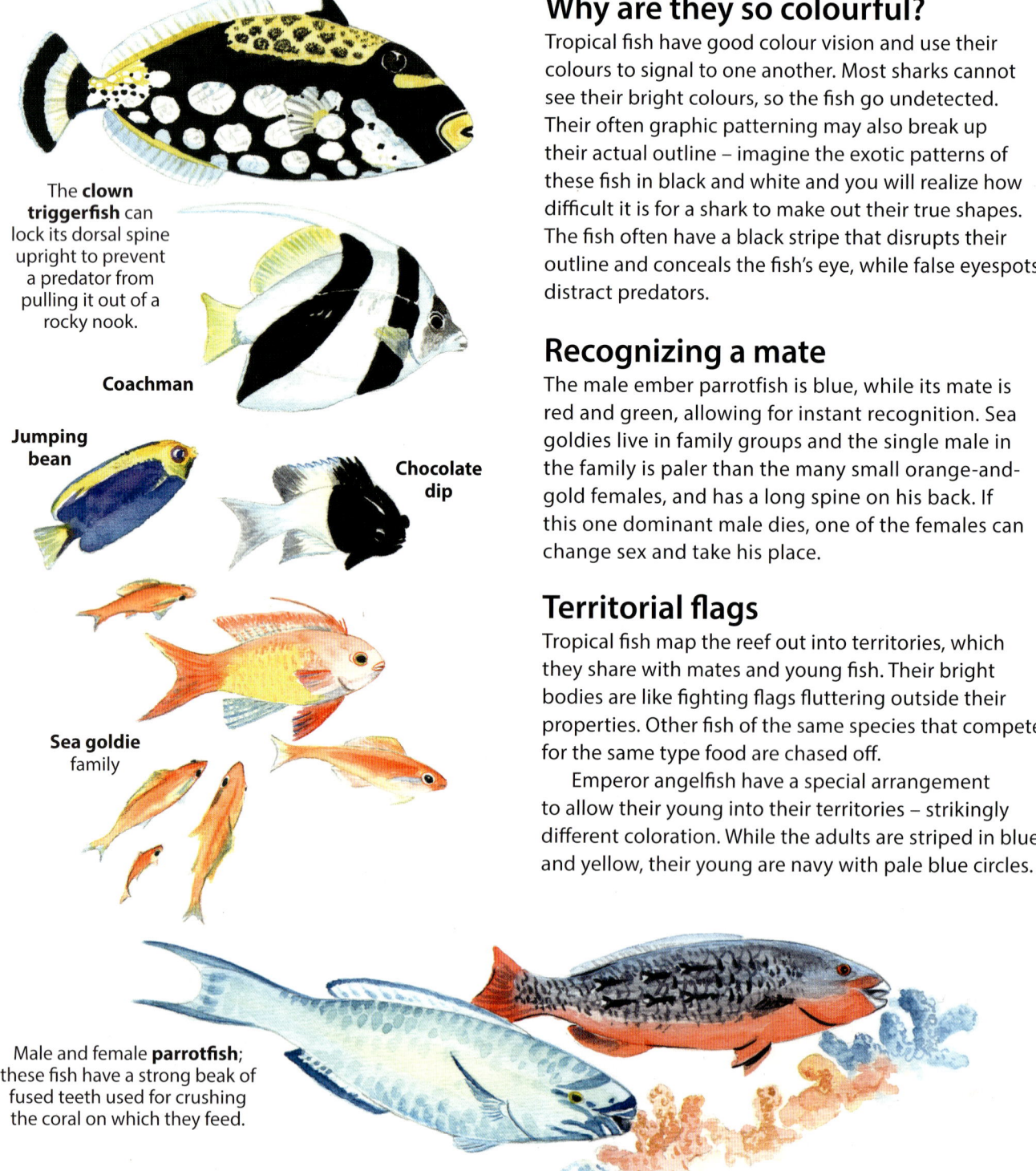

The **clown triggerfish** can lock its dorsal spine upright to prevent a predator from pulling it out of a rocky nook.

Coachman

Jumping bean

Chocolate dip

Sea goldie family

Male and female **parrotfish**; these fish have a strong beak of fused teeth used for crushing the coral on which they feed.

Why are they so colourful?

Tropical fish have good colour vision and use their colours to signal to one another. Most sharks cannot see their bright colours, so the fish go undetected. Their often graphic patterning may also break up their actual outline – imagine the exotic patterns of these fish in black and white and you will realize how difficult it is for a shark to make out their true shapes. The fish often have a black stripe that disrupts their outline and conceals the fish's eye, while false eyespots distract predators.

Recognizing a mate

The male ember parrotfish is blue, while its mate is red and green, allowing for instant recognition. Sea goldies live in family groups and the single male in the family is paler than the many small orange-and-gold females, and has a long spine on his back. If this one dominant male dies, one of the females can change sex and take his place.

Territorial flags

Tropical fish map the reef out into territories, which they share with mates and young fish. Their bright bodies are like fighting flags fluttering outside their properties. Other fish of the same species that compete for the same type food are chased off.

Emperor angelfish have a special arrangement to allow their young into their territories – strikingly different coloration. While the adults are striped in blue and yellow, their young are navy with pale blue circles.

> **Things to do**
> - Visit an aquarium to see some of these tropical fish.
> - For a real treat, snorkel on a coral reef.

Warning of danger

Sometimes distinctive colours and patterns warn that an animal is dangerous. The devil firefish on page 41 is a good example. The powder-blue surgeon has a razor-sharp spine on the side of the tail, which is extended to slash its enemies. The bright yellow fin and yellow stripe around the spine serve as a warning.

Shaped for success

The strange shapes of tropical fish enable them to move in and out of the coral and collect food from unusual places (see the long-nosed butterflyfish, page 39). These fish can move and turn in tight spaces, but they cannot escape quickly, so they release poisons when frightened.

Colours for camouflage

The bright rainbow wrasse waits quietly among colourful seaweeds and captures crabs, worms and small fish. Rock cods lurk in caves and capture fish with their big mouths. They come in many different colours that help them to blend into the background.

Advertising useful services

The famous bluestreak cleaner wrasse works unharmed on dangerous fish, performing an important health service by eating parasites and cleaning wounds. It flutters its fins and does an unusual dance to advertise its cleaning services. The sabre-toothed blenny copies the cleaner fish, but instead of cleaning other fish it snatches a surprise bite!

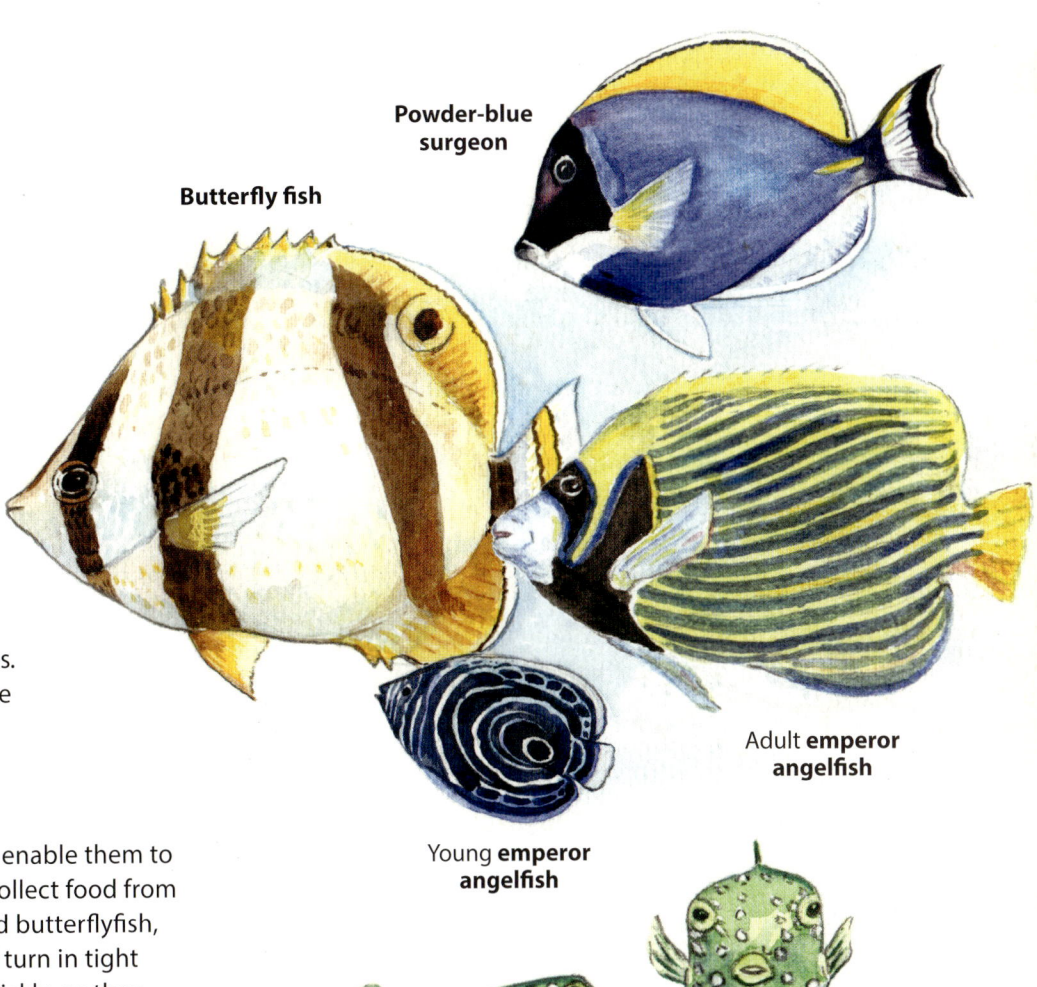

Powder-blue surgeon

Butterfly fish

Adult **emperor angelfish**

Young **emperor angelfish**

Rainbow wrasse

Boxfish have a stiff armour of fused scales.

Freckled hawkfish coloured for camouflage

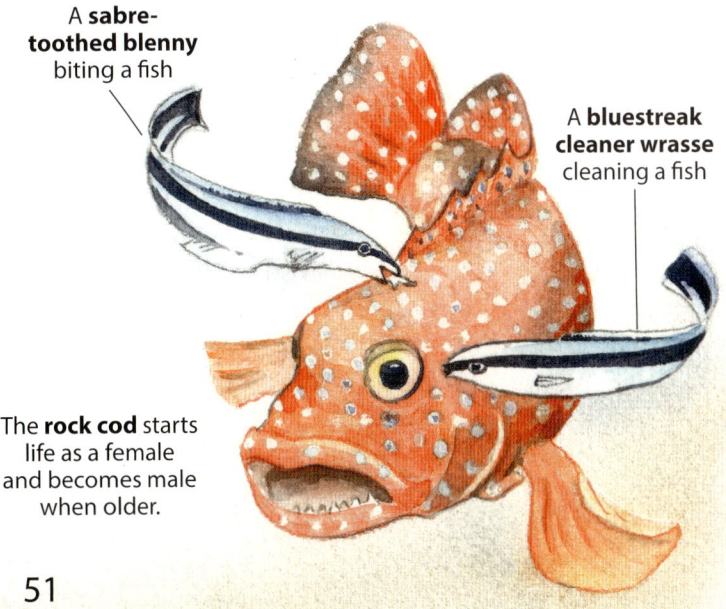

A **sabre-toothed blenny** biting a fish

A **bluestreak cleaner wrasse** cleaning a fish

The **rock cod** starts life as a female and becomes male when older.

Diving deeper

Sharks, rays and skates

There are hundreds of different sharks, rays and skates in the ocean, and they have ancient origins: sharks, for example, have been major predators for over 350 million years.

Zambezi sharks are considered dangerous to humans.

No bones!

Unlike bony fish, sharks, rays and skates have skeletons made of cartilage. Instead of scales they have rather rough skin with little teeth embedded in it. They have five to seven gill slits on each side of the body and they lack swim bladders. In sharks, the lateral fins prevent them from nose-diving to the bottom, and the oil in their large livers gives them buoyancy.

Shaped for life

Many sharks are streamlined for swimming quickly through open water when hunting, but not all sharks need to move that fast. Catsharks and shysharks, for instance, are reef dwellers and are built for moving in and out of nooks and crannies to catch an octopus or crab. The bottom-dwelling sandsharks, rays and skates are flat and lie on the seabed or glide gracefully through the water. They ambush and snuffle for prey in the sand, grinding fish and shellfish with their flattened teeth. Their mouths and gill openings are beneath their bodies and could get clogged with sand, but there is a hole behind each eye, called the spiracle, where water enters from above to aerate the gills. The weird sawfish has a long jagged snout to slash at prey.

The gentle giant

The enormous whale shark is not a dangerous predator but a filter feeder! This spotted giant has a broad, flat head and swims with its huge mouth open, sieving water through its gills to trap the great quantity of plankton and coral eggs that its body needs.

Shark births and mermaid's purses

Rays and most sharks have eggs that hatch and develop inside the mother. The babies are born in shallow water. Catsharks, skates and St Joseph sharks lay horny egg cases, known as mermaids' purses, which can sometimes be found washed up on the beach.

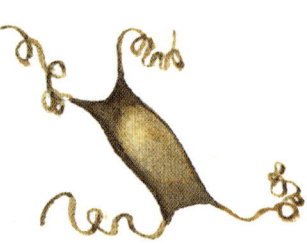

Mermaid's purse

Electric rays stun their prey with a powerful electric shock, so take care not to tread on one!

Hammerhead shark

Pyjama catshark

St Joseph shark

Stingray undersurface

Stingray upper surface

The **sawfish** lashes at prey with its saw.

Sandshark

Efficient predators

Many sharks are streamlined killing machines. They find their prey by using finely tuned senses like eyesight, smell, and the electricity-detecting organs around the nose, and then attack with a burst of speed. Their fearsome jaws have several rows of jagged teeth, with spares ready to replace any that are lost. The Zambezi shark can tolerate fresh water and enters rivers, swimming up to 100 kilometres inland. The eyes and nostrils of the hammerhead shark are on the sides of its strange head. It has an exceptional sense of smell and can detect blood several kilometres away.

Great white shark

The great white shark, with its pointed snout and black eyes, is the most efficient predator of all sharks. In spite of their reputation as being dangerous to humans, these sharks play a vital role as top predators in the ocean ecosystem. Too many were being killed by trophy hunters, causing an international outcry. South Africa was the first country to protect great whites by law.

Did you know?
One tagged great white shark swam over 20,000km to Australia and back in nine months.

Gill slits

Great white sharks can reach 6m in length and weigh up to 1,200kg.

How to treat a shark-bite victim

Stay calm and call for medical help. Control the bleeding by pressing on the wound with a wad of material. The victim should lie head lower than body, and be kept warm. To help with the shock reassure the victim. Don't give him or her anything to drink.

Bather safety

Most shark attacks have occurred along the east coast of South Africa. In KwaZulu-Natal (KZN), nets to safeguard swimmers are laid in two overlapping rows, but do not form a continuous barrier to keep the sharks out. They act more as traps. This is effective at reducing the number of sharks near the shore, but is not ideal, as the nets catch not only sharks but also dolphins and turtles. The KZN Sharks Board removes and releases animals caught in the nets. Baited hooks attached to floating drums are also used to catch sharks, while sparing dolphins.

At Fish Hoek in Cape Town a fine mesh net is used to keep sharks out of the bathing area without killing them – or other marine animals. Shark spotters are also stationed on the mountains above False Bay and use binoculars to look out for sharks. If a shark is spotted, they radio to the beach below. Bathers are then warned to leave the water by means of a siren and a white flag with a black shark on it.

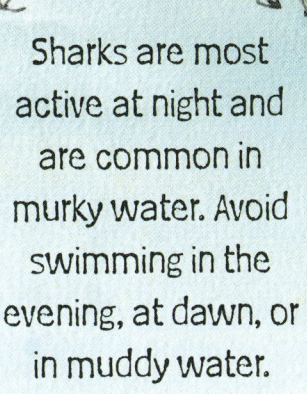

Sharks are most active at night and are common in murky water. Avoid swimming in the evening, at dawn, or in muddy water.

Diving deeper

Sea birds

You can have hours of fun watching birds, especially if you use a pair of binoculars. Most birds can fly. Their bones are hollow but strong and have special air cells to make them light. The feathers are also light and flexible.

A Hartlaub's gull using the wind to give it a lift

Things to do
- Watch sea birds flying. How do they use their wings, tail and feet for take-off and landing? Why do you think most sea birds are black and white?
- Fly a kite. This will give you an idea of how seagulls use air currents to stay in the air.

Comical penguins

African penguins are not able to fly. They waddle over the rocks on their short legs and big webbed feet. Yet they are graceful swimmers, darting after fish, and using their wings and feet like flippers. The first bird to dive in is often in danger of being caught by a lurking seal. The penguins push and shove one another until one falls in and, if he is unharmed, the rest join him. They keep together for safety and to herd fish. Their short feathers make a warm waterproof coat. Once a year they moult and have to stay ashore until their new feathers have grown, so during this time they cannot fish for food. Penguins nest in burrows or among rocks and have one or two fluffy brown chicks.

Scavenging seagulls

Seagulls are scavengers and have learnt to follow fishing boats, where they squabble over the fish guts that are thrown out. They will even grab scraps from a feeding shark! The large kelp gull (shown on page 8) has a red spot on its yellow bill. The hungry chicks peck this spot to make the adult bring up food for them from its own stomach. Young kelp gulls are a mottled brown colour. Hartlaub's gulls (like that shown above) are smaller than kelp gulls, with grey-and-black wings. They look similar to another gull, the grey-headed gull, which occurs on the east coast.

Conservation of coastal birds

In Cape Town you can visit SANCCOB, where birds damaged by oil pollution are cleaned and fed until they can be released. Abandoned eggs are hatched and the chicks are hand reared. In 2000 more than 20,000 penguins were rescued by various organizations and volunteers after the ship *Treasure* sank off Blouberg and spilt a lot of oil.

The Cape also has two protected wild African Penguin colonies – one at Boulders Beach on the Cape Peninsula and the other at Stony Point in Betty's Bay.

The African penguin occurs only around southern Africa. It has become endangered and could go extinct if not protected.

> ### Did you know?
> Bird islands are usually protected to allow the birds to breed undisturbed. But at Lambert's Bay you can cross the harbour breakwater to a small island. Once you have got used to the smell of their droppings (guano), you can enjoy the spectacle of masses of breeding sea birds.

A safe nesting place

You may think that the cormorant's nest in the photo on the right is perched rather dangerously high on the rocks. But up there it is safe from enemies like jackals, mongooses, rats and snakes. Adult birds launch themselves into flight from these cliff tops quite easily – like hang gliders. You may see flocks of these black birds strung across the sky or diving and following a shoal of fish.

A weight belt with wings!

The cormorant's wings are not waterproof. When wet, their extra weight helps the cormorant to dive deeper (like a diver's weight belt). After a dive they hold their wings out to dry in the breeze.

Cormorants nest on high, exposed rocks.

A gannet points its beak skywards as it walks through the crowded colony. Look for the fluffy white chicks and young dark grey birds.

Gannet colonies

Gannets are graceful birds and can fly hundreds of kilometres in a day. When they spot a shoal of fish they tuck back their wings and drop down with their sharp beaks, entering the water like knives, point down. The impact of these large birds hitting the water is softened by air cushions at the base of their neck. They have no outside nostrils where water could rush in.

Finding food

Like many sea birds, gannets nest in colonies on islands, where they are safe from predators. Each pair jealously guards its nest, which is a hollow in a mound of guano (bird droppings.) The female lays just one egg, and the parents take turns at keeping it warm with their webbed feet.

A runway for take-off

At the side of the gannet colony is a runway where the large birds can build up enough speed for liftoff. When a bird walks through the crowded colony to the runway, it is in danger of being pecked. It points its beak to the sky as if to say 'I won't attack, just let me pass'. When a bird lands back at its nest, it bows to its mate and they cross their necks first to one side and then the other. This helps them to recognize each other in these crowded conditions.

Diving deeper

Marine mammals

Whales, dolphins and seals are the mammals of the sea. They breathe air (whales and dolphins do this through blowholes on the top of their head) and give birth to young, which are suckled by their mothers.

Winter visitors – southern rights

Every winter southern right whales migrate from their Antarctic feeding grounds to breed off the coast of South Africa. You may see their huge tails lifting out of the water or hear them puffing air from their blowholes. Whales are not fish, even though they may look like them. They are actually warm-blooded mammals, rather like swimming elephants. They can grow many times bigger than an elephant because the water supports their weight. Beneath their smooth skin is a thick layer of fatty blubber, which helps the whale to float and keeps it warm in icy water.

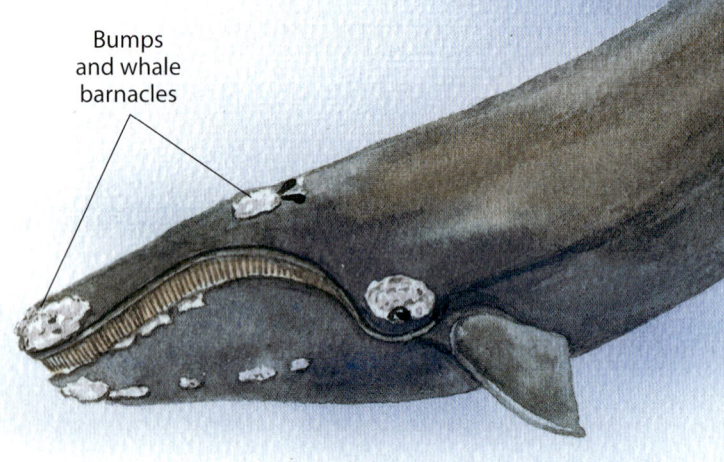

Bumps and whale barnacles

The **southern right whale** is the most common whale that visits the coast of South Africa. It is a baleen whale with a smooth throat and no dorsal fin.

Baleen feeders

You will not easily see adult whales feeding unless you travel to the icy Antarctic where they eat krill shrimps. Instead of teeth, most whales have horny combs with hairs hanging from their top jaws. These are called baleen plates. These whales gulp in water and squirt it out through the baleen hairs, which trap the krill. So some of the largest living creatures are filter feeders, eating some of the smallest creatures!

Whale births

Southern right whales come into sheltered bays to mate and give birth between June and November. It is exciting to see these big creatures leaping out of the water and landing with a splash as they show off to their mates. A baby whale (calf) is born tail-first so that it does not drown. It is lifted to the surface by its mother, and takes its first breath. Because it cannot suck under water, milk is squirted into its mouth from the nipples beneath the mother's belly.

Air breathers

Although whales breathe air, they can dive hundreds of metres deep and stay under water for up to an hour. During the dive their lungs collapse, and the oxygen needed for energy is obtained from their blood and muscles, rather than from air. This prevents them from getting 'the bends', a dangerous condition in which gas bubbles form in the blood when a diver rises up from deep water too quickly.

Echo-location

Whales and dolphins find their way by echo-location: they make high-pitched clicks, and the soundwaves bounce off solid objects sending echoes back to their ears, which tell them how close the rocks are and how deep the water is. Dolphins and whales are very sociable and communicate with each other with clicks and songs. Some of their sounds are beyond the range of our hearing, but can be louder than the roar of a jet and are heard by other whales many kilometres away.

Things to do
- Visit the giant whale displays at the Iziko Museum in Cape Town.
- Hike the Whale Trail at De Hoop Nature Reserve.

Bottlenose dolphins often frolic in the waves and hunt in packs.

Toothed whales

The toothed whales are predators and include dolphins, square-headed sperm whales and black-and-white killer whales (orcas). They use their teeth to capture squid, fish and young seals and swallow them whole.

The Cape fur seal

Seals are rather like swimming dogs. For protection and warmth they have a layer of fatty blubber under the skin and a thick coat of fur. Their legs have become flippers and although they hump and slither clumsily over the rocks, they are swift swimmers. They can stay in the water for days at a time but must come ashore to mate, give birth and moult. In October, the males haul themselves onto islands and deserted shores, where they establish territories. Pregnant females arrive next and give birth to squealing black pups. The pups live off the mother's rich milk. They play, explore and learn to swim. When they are several months old they can start to catch their own fish and squid. Soon after giving birth the females are ready to mate again, and the next generation of pups is born a year later, when the seals return to their breeding colony.

Conservation

For centuries whales and seals were hunted to obtain oil, baleen, meat and furs. Their numbers declined until some whales almost became extinct, causing a public outcry about the slaughter. Many countries then co-operated in passing international laws to protect whales, and their populations have now increased again. Seals are protected in South Africa even though they are not endangered. Fishermen find them a nuisance when they feast on fish, depleting stocks for the fishermen, and damage fishing nets.

Cape fur seals – the largest seal colonies in the world occur on the west coast of southern Africa.

The bigger picture

Contrasting life in two oceans

Southern Africa's coast is pounded by the Indian Ocean to the east and the Atlantic Ocean to the west. Cape Agulhas is the southernmost tip of Africa, while Cape Point is the division between the south and west coasts, with distinct sea life and different sea temperatures on either side of the

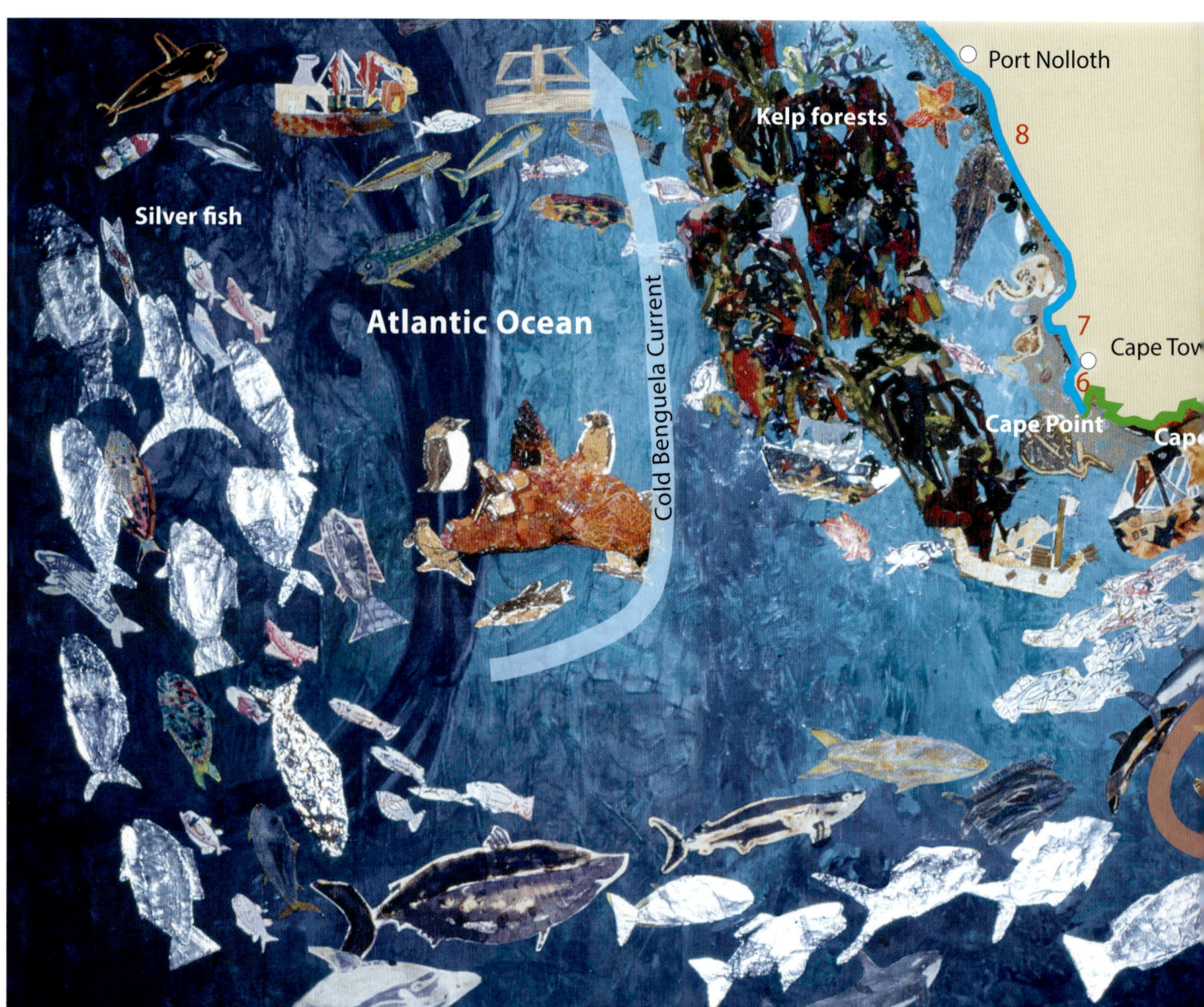

Things to do

Create a mural like this giant one made by over 100 children from Cape Town. The children used a variety of techniques, and added shells, sand, and even a few shipwrecks off Cape Agulhas.

West coast (9–15 °C)

The Benguela Current flows northwards along the west coast, bringing cold water from the south. When a southeasterly wind blows surface water offshore, icy-cold water wells up to replace it. This brings nutrients up from the seafloor. Plant plankton and kelp forests grow in the rich water and provide a vast food supply. This food supports enormous numbers of animals, but not many different species. These include silvery schooling fish, hake, mussels, limpets, rock lobsters and seals. Many people make a living by harvesting kelp, fish and shellfish.

Cape Peninsula. Look at the following mural showing how sea life differs around South Africa. There are three coastal regions (west, south and east) with different sea temperatures, resulting in different kinds of sea life and climates.

> **Things to do**
>
> Areas 1–8 on the map are special marine reserves known as 'marine protected areas'. See pages 60–61 for details.

South coast (16–21°C)
The south coast is an intermediate region where the Agulhas Current travels further offshore. There are many seaweeds there, but few kelps. In winter, sardines migrate through this region up to the east coast and are followed by larger fish, sharks and dolphins.

East coast (22–27°C)
The powerful Agulhas Current flows southwards along the east coast bringing warm clear water from the tropics, with low levels of nutrients and very little plant plankton. The seaweeds are small and often contain lime or chemicals to deter grazers. There are many different animal species: herbivores compete for the scarce seaweed food, and there are numerous carnivores, making it a dangerous place in which to live.

The bigger picture

Conservation

In your grandparents' time there was so much life in the sea that they could easily collect delicious seafood. But today it is much harder to find rock lobsters, oysters, abalone or mussels, and many types of fish have dropped to less than one twentieth of their original numbers.

What happened to the seafood?

Cape Town's population has grown from 1 million to 4 million people in just 25 years, while the population of South Africa has increased from about 17 million to 57 million in 60 years. In fact, throughout the world human populations have grown so large that we have overfished to meet our demand for food, and the size of many fish populations has decreased dramatically.

What can be done?

We must either reduce the rate at which our population is increasing or allow marine life to reproduce sufficiently to replace what we are taking from the sea.

The riches of the sea are living resources and can grow and reproduce just like humans do. In fact fish, rock lobsters and mussels produce millions of eggs that could grow up into adults in just a few years. We can save our living resources by harvesting them sustainably – this means we must leave enough adults to reproduce and also protect the juveniles and larvae.

Control measures

You need a licence to fish: this controls the numbers and activities of people wanting to participate.

There are regulations on the numbers and sizes of fish that can be caught. You may not catch endangered fish, and you may not catch certain species during their breeding seasons.

Marine protected areas (MPAs)

One of the best ways for a country to conserve marine life is to set aside marine reserves where the marine life can breed and grow, safe from harvesters. Because there are no fences in the ocean, active animals like fish, and the larvae of sedentary animals such as mussels and abalone, can still move out of a reserve and stock other areas nearby. So fish and fishermen both benefit from protected areas.

Did you know?

Turtles are critically endangered. They are protected on our shores but are still harvested in other countries. They get caught in fishing nets and also suffer because of plastic pollution.

The turtle is not sad: tears run from her eyes to get rid of the salt in the water she swallowed when eating crabs, whelks, clams and urchins.

A **loggerhead turtle** lays about 150 eggs in its nest in the sand dunes.

The huge **leatherback turtle** slurps up jellyfish prey. Plastic bags look just like jellyfish, but they are killer 'foods': so don't litter. Plastic bags thoughtlessly dropped on land can be blown or washed into the ocean.

Nesting turtles at iSimangaliso Wetland Park

Marine turtles spend most of their lives travelling the ocean. They swim great distances using their flippers. After mating, female turtles return to their home beaches in summer. They lumber ashore, dig a hole, fill it with eggs, and then laboriously cover it with sand. About 60 nights later the hatchlings emerge – if the nest was hot (29°C) most of them are females, but if it was cooler they are mainly males.

Since they were first protected on the east coast, the number of nesting leatherback turtles has increased from 50 to 400, and the number of nesting loggerheads has increased from 400 to almost 4,000.

Things to do

- In South Africa you can visit one of these popular MPAs, numbered 1–8 on pages 58–59:
    1. iSimangaliso Wetland Park,
    2. Addo Elephant National Park
    3. Tsitsikamma National Park
    4. Garden Route National Park
    5. Agulhas National Park
    6. Table Mountain National Park
    7. West Coast National Park
    8. Namaqua National Park.
- Other protected areas include: Stilbaai, Goukamma, Robberg, De Hoop, Betty's Bay, Rocherpan, Aliwal Shoal and Pondoland.
- To the north, the Namibian Islands' MPA and a network of reserves in Mozambique, including the Ponta do Ouro Partial Marine Reserve and the extensive Primeiras and Segundas Islands Environmental Protected Area, also help to conserve marine life.

Loggerhead hatchlings scurry for the sea to escape predatory ghost crabs, gulls and mongooses. Lurking fish and sharks also pose a danger once the hatchlings reach the water.

Things to do

In summer, join a night tour to see the turtles laying or hatching.

Useful contacts

Many of these organizations produce excellent magazines and teaching aids.

BAYWORLD OCEANARIUM
www.bayworld.co.za
PO Box 13147
Humewood
Port Elizabeth, 6013
Tel: (041) 584 0650

BARTOLOMEU DIAS
MUSEUM COMPLEX
www.diasmuseum.co.za
1 Market Street
Mossel Bay, 6500
Tel: (044) 691 1067

CAPENATURE
www.capenature.co.za
Private Bag X9086
Cape Town, 8000
Tel: (021) 483 0000

DEPARTMENT OF AGRICULTURE,
FORESTRY AND FISHERIES (DAFF)
www.daff.gov.za
Private Bag X9087
Cape Town, 8000
Tel: (012) 319 6000

DEPARTMENT OF ENVIRONMENTAL
AFFAIRS AND TOURISM (DEAT)
www.environment.gov.za
473 Steve Biko Road, Arcadia
Pretoria, 0083
Tel: (021) 441 2700

EZEMVELO KZN WILDLIFE
www.ekznw.co.za
Peter Brown Drive
Town Bush Valley
Pietermaritzburg, 3202
Tel: (033) 845 1000

IZIKO SOUTH AFRICAN MUSEUM
www.iziko.org.za
25 Victoria Street
Cape Town, 8001
Tel: (021) 481 3800

SANCCOB (SA FOUNDATION
FOR THE CONSERVATION OF
COASTAL BIRDS)
www.sanccob.co.za
PO Box 1116,
Bloubergrant, 7443
Tel: (021) 557 6155

SOUTH AFRICAN NATIONAL PARKS
(SANPARKS)
www.sanparks.org
E-mail: reservations@parks-sa.co.za
Tel: (012) 428 9111

TWO OCEANS AQUARIUM
PO Box 50603,
Waterfront, 8001
Tel: (021) 418 3823

USHAKA MARINE WORLD
www.ushakamarineworld.co.za
1 King Shaka Avenue
Durban, 4001
Tel: (031) 328 8222

WILDLIFE AND ENVIRONMENTAL
SOCIETY OF SOUTH AFRICA (WESSA)
www.wessa.org.za
Tel: (0332) 30391 (branches nationwide)

WWF SOUTH AFRICA (WORLD WIDE
FUND FOR NATURE)
www.wwf.org.za
PO Box 23273
Claremont, 7735
Tel: (021) 657 6600

Useful references

The **porcupinefish** blows itself into a prickly ball if threatened.

Branch, GM, Griffiths, CL, Branch, ML and Beckley, LE. 2016. *Two Oceans: A guide to the marine life of southern Africa*. Struik Nature, Cape Town.

Branch, GM and Branch, ML. 2018. *Living Shores: Interacting with marine ecosystems in southern Africa*. Struik Nature, Cape Town.

Payne, AIL and Crawford, RJM (eds). 1989. *Oceans of Life off Southern Africa*. Vlaeberg Publishers, Cape Town.

Von der Heyden, S. 2012 *Southern African Sea Life: A guide for young explorers*. Struik Nature, Cape Town.

Key words

Agulhas Current The warm current in the Indian Ocean that flows south down the east coast of South Africa

Algae (sing. alga) Simple non-flowering water plants such as seaweed and phytoplankton

Arthropod An invertebrate animal with a segmented body, jointed limbs and an external skeleton, such as an insect, spider, crab or prawn

Bacteria Microscopic, single-celled organisms without a nucleus, some of which can cause decay or disease

Baleen Comb-like plates that hang from the top jaw in certain whales, used for filtering food from water

Benguela Current The cold current in the Atlantic Ocean that flows northward along the west coast of South Africa towards the tropics

Biological clock The built-in control of rhythmic activities in plants and animals

Calcium carbonate (limestone, chalk) A hard white compound found in bones, shells and coral skeletons

Camouflage Blending in with the colours and shapes of the natural surrounding and hence difficult to see

Carnivore An animal that eats other animals

Cartilage (gristle) A firm elastic tissue that forms all or part of the vertebrate skeleton

Chlorophyll The green pigment found in most plants and responsible for light absorption to provide energy for photosynthesis

Echo-sounder A sounding apparatus for determining the depth of objects beneath a ship by measuring the time taken for an echo to bounce back from objects such as the seafloor or shoals of fish

Ecosystem A community of living things that interact with one another and their physical environment

Environment The physical surroundings and conditions in which things live

Filter feed To sieve small food particles from the water

Gill The organ in fish and other aquatic animals used to take up oxygen from the water and remove carbon dioxide during respiration

Grazer An animal that feeds on growing plants

Habitat The natural home of an animal or plant

Herbivore An animal that feeds on plants

Intertidal Between the high-tide and low-tide levels on the shore

Invertebrate An animal with no backbone or spine

Larva (pl. larvae) Juvenile form of an animal that looks different from the adult

Mammal A warm-blooded vertebrate usually with hair or fur. The young develop inside the mother, are born, and suckle on milk. Examples are humans, seals and whales.

Nutrient Any substance that provides essential nourishment for the maintenance of life and growth

Organism A living individual, which may be a single cell or a many-celled plant or animal

Parasite An organism living in or on another and benefiting at the expense of its host

Photosynthesis The process by which plants use green chlorophyll to absorb the energy of sunlight and use it to convert carbon dioxide and water into simple sugars for food

Plankton The chiefly microscopic organisms that drift in the sea or fresh water; can consist of plants (phytoplankton) or animals (zooplankton)

Pollution Unwanted, harmful chemicals or materials contaminating the environment

Polyp A simple animal with a cup-shaped body and a mouth usually surrounded by tentacles

Predator An animal that preys on other animals

Primary producer A plant that produces energy-rich food from non-living substances and comprise the first stage in any food chain. Examples are seaweeds and phytoplankton, which produce food from water and carbon dioxide.

Reproduce To produce offspring

Respiration The act of breathing; in living organisms, the process involving the release of energy and carbon dioxide from the breakdown of organic substances

Sedentary Stationary or slow-moving

Shoal A number of fish swimming together (also called a school)

Skeleton A hard internal or external framework that supports the body of an animal; made from bone, cartilage, shell or fibres

Spore A reproductive cell produced by micro-organisms and plants that don't have seeds

Swim bladder A gas-filled sac in fishes used to maintain buoyancy

Territory An area defended by an animal against others

Venom A poisonous fluid secreted by animals such as snakes or stonefish, usually injected by a sting or bite

Vertebrate Any animal with a spinal column or backbone; examples are mammals, birds, reptiles, amphibians and fish

Zonation Well-defined regions (especially between low- and high-tide levels) with particular plants, animals and physical features

Index

abalone 29
air bladder 23
algae (see seaweed) 25, 34, 44
amphipod 30
anemone 18–19, 21, 25, 32, 34–35
Atlantic Ocean 4, 58–59

baleen 56–57
barnacle 18–21, 28
basket-star 37
beach hopper 9
birds 8–9, 20–21, 54–55
bivalve 12
blubber 56, 57
bluebottle 6, 34, 40–41
brittle-star 30, 37
bubble-raft shell 6
bubble shell 12, 13, 19, 32
by-the-wind sailor 7

calamari 15
camouflage 33, 37, 41
cartilage 52
catshark 52
cephalopods 14
chitons 12, 23
clam 25, 45
clownfish 35
clown shrimp 30
Cnidaria 34
coelacanth 48
cone shell 25
coral 34, 35, 50–51
cormorants 55
cowries 12–13, 27
crabs
    boxer 35
    fiddler 10
    ghost 11
    hermit 28
    mole 11
    rock 17
    seaweed 30
    sponge 28
    swimming 10
crayfish – see rock lobster
Crustacea 28

cuttlefish 12–13, 14–16

devil firefish 41
dolphin 57

ear shell 12, 24
east coast 11, 18–19, 26–27, 34, 39, 40, 47, 50, 53, 54, 59, 61, 63
echinoderms 38–39
echo-location 57
electric ray 52

feather hydroids 35
feather stars 37
filter feeders 8, 12, 21, 42–45, 56
fish 46–53
food chain 15, 22, 44

gannets 55
gill 8, 10, 11, 12, 13, 16, 24, 32, 33, 36, 39, 44, 47, 48, 52, 53
gill rakers 44, 47
guano 55
gulls 8, 54

hagfish 48
hammerhead shark 52
helmet shell 24
herbivore 22–23, 59
hermit crab 28

Indian Ocean 4, 58–59
invertebrate 15

jellyfish 6, 7, 34, 40, 49, 61

kelp 4, 9, 23, 38, 42–43, 58–59
krill 56

larvae 20, 21, 28, 29, 37, 60
limpet 12, 18–21, 23–26, 30, 36, 43, 58
littorina see periwinkle

mammals 56–57

mantle 13, 17, 25, 27
mantle cavity 17
mermaid's purse 52
molluscs 13, 14, 16, 23, 26, 28, 32, 36
moray eel 29
moult 10, 11, 28, 29, 36, 38, 54, 57
mudhopper 48
mussels 8, 10, 18, 21, 25, 26, 29, 36, 43, 44, 45, 58, 60

nudibranch 32–33

octopus 12, 14, 16–17, 26, 27, 29, 43, 47, 52
oyster 18, 19, 21, 26, 45, 60
oystercatcher 21, 26

pansy shell 39
paper nautilus 16
penguin 54
periwinkle 18–20
perlemoen see abalone 23, 43
phytoplankton 44–45
plankton 8, 44–45
plough shell 8, 10, 15, 26
polyps 6, 34–35
prawns 28–29
pufferfish 41

ram's-horn shell 14, 15
redbait 18–19, 24, 36, 43, 47
red tide 44–45
rock lobster 28–29, 45

sardine 44, 46–47, 58–59
sea cucumber 38–39
sea fans 35
sea hare 33
seahorse 30, 49
seal 56–57
sea lice 9, 30, 43
sea slug (see nudibranch) 7, 32–33, 35
sea spider 30
sea stars 36–37

sea swallow 7
sea urchin 38–39
seaweed 18–19, 22–23, 42–43
shark 52–53
shark nets 53
shark victim treatment 53
shells
    mollusc 12–13
    crab 10–11, 28
    urchin 38–39
shrimps 14–15, 28–29
siphon 8, 14, 16
snails (see molluscs) 24–25
soft corals 35
south coast 58–59
sponge 18–19, 28, 40
squid 14–15
starfish 36–37
stinging cells 6–7, 32, 34–35
stingray 52
stonefish 41
swim bladder 46

tentacle 6–7, 14–15, 34–35, 39
tides 18–23, 32
tube feet 36–38

urchin 38–39

vertebrates 46–59

west coast 13, 19, 26, 29, 42, 45, 57, 58–59
whale 56
whelk 12–13, 24–27, 29
white-fronted plover 9
winkle 12–13, 18–19, 23
worms
    fan 30
    fire- 40
    flat- 30
    reef 20–21

zoanthids 18–19, 25, 34–35
zooplankton 44